Doubting Vision

Doubting Vision

Film and the Revelationist Tradition

Malcolm Turvey

OXFORD

UNIVERSITY PRESS

2008

OXFORD
UNIVERSITY PRESS

Oxford University Press, Inc., publishes works that further
Oxford University's objective of excellence
in research, scholarship, and education.

Oxford   New York
Auckland   Bangkok   Bogotá   Buenos Aires   Cape Town   Chennai
Dar es Salaam   Delhi   Hong Kong   Istanbul   Karachi   Kolkata
Kuala Lumpur   Madrid   Melbourne   Mexico City   Mumbai   Nairobi
São Paulo   Shanghai   Singapore   Taipei   Tokyo   Toronto

Published by Oxford University Press, Inc.
198 Madison Avenue, New York, New York, 10016

www.oup.com

Library of Congress Cataloging-in-Publication Data

Turvey, Malcolm, 1969–
Doubting vision : film and the revelationist tradition / by Malcolm Turvey.
p. cm.
Includes bibliographical references and index.
ISBN 978-0-19-532097-8; 978-0-19-532098-5 (pbk.)
1. Film criticism—Europe—History.   I. Title.
PN1995.T7935 2008
791.4301—dc22   2007043642

9 8 7 6 5 4 3 2 1

Printed in the United States of America
on acid-free paper

To my father, George Henry Turvey, and in memory
of my mother, Lorna Lesley Turvey

The concept of "seeing" makes a tangled impression. Well, it is tangled.

—Ludwig Wittgenstein, *Philosophical Investigations*

ACKNOWLEDGMENTS

This book originated in a Ph.D. dissertation under the supervision of Richard Allen in the cinema studies department at New York University. I thank him as well as the other members of my committee, Annette Michelson, Stuart Liebman, Noël Carroll, and William Simon. Stuart kindly recommended the project to Oxford University Press, and his dissertation on Jean Epstein's early film theory has had a major influence on my thinking about Epstein.

While completing the dissertation, I taught for a year in the communication arts department at the University of Wisconsin, Madison, where I was welcomed warmly by faculty, staff, and students. In particular I thank my teaching assistant, Jane M. Greene, for her friendship and support. I also encountered two formidable thinkers who made me realize (perhaps unbeknownst to them) that I needed to fundamentally reconceptualize this project. Noël Carroll carefully read and criticized the first version of the manuscript, exposing its theoretical flaws in the kindest way possible, while David Bordwell brought home to me the limits of theoretical explanation. Both also proved to be generous, supportive, and fun colleagues. While the rewriting that ensued was a time-consuming and at times painful process, I think the dissertation, and the subsequent book, is much better for it. I hope they agree.

For the past ten years I have been fortunate to be associated with the journal *October,* and I thank its editors, Annette Michelson, Rosalind Krauss, Yve-Alain Bois, Benjamin Buchloh, Hal Foster, Denis Hollier, George Baker, and Mignon Nixon, for lively and stimulating intellectual exchange. In particular I must acknowledge Rosalind, who has not only been unfailingly generous over the years, but whose seminal book *The Optical Unconscious* first alerted me to the role of visual skepticism in modernism.

I'm grateful to those anonymous reviewers who encouraged me to address contemporary film theory and to better justify my theoretical approach. Conversations with Murray Smith and Federico Windhausen have helped in too many ways to mention. I thank my colleagues in visual culture at Sarah Lawrence College, as well as Bella Brodzki, Gilberto Perez, Shahnaz Rouse, and Maria Negroni, whose dedication to their own scholarship has been an inspiration. Thanks also to my students and research assistants, especially Hillary Plemons. Two Bogert grants from Sarah Lawrence College for release time from teaching helped me complete the book.

I thank my editor at Oxford University Press, Shannon McLachlan, for taking a chance on a work of film theory at a time when university presses show too little interest in the subject, as well as Christina Gibson and Gwen Colvin for their help in steering the book through production.

Most important, I thank my intellectual mentors, Annette Michelson and Richard Allen. Annette's courses and articles on film theory, avant-garde film, and the visual arts fired my imagination while a graduate student unlike anything before. Richard showed me a new way of thinking and writing, one in which clarity, precision, conceptual delineation, and a suspicion of a priori generalization are the hallmarks. The example of their work has at all times been in the forefront of my mind while writing this book.

The book's publication coincides with the tenth year of my membership in the Brooklyn Symphony Orchestra. The music I have played in the orchestra, along with the friends I have made while doing so, have enriched my life in ways academia cannot.

I thank Tony and Susan Pasquariello for their support, good humor, and the endless diversion of playing Philadelphia rummy. My wife, Lisa, is a better writer than I could ever hope to be. She has painstakingly read every word, correcting my grammatical mistakes and suggesting graceful alternatives to my awkward phrasing. Much more important, she makes my life better every day.

Finally, the love of my family has sustained me through my work on this project. I have wonderful memories of watching movies with my parents while growing up, and the genuine pleasure they took in film led me to study it. This book is dedicated to them.

CONTENTS

Doubting Vision

Introduction

I

The major goal of film theory before the 1960s—what today is known as "classical" film theory—was to prove that the cinema is an art on a par with, or perhaps even superior to, the other arts.[1] Due to its novelty, the prejudice against its photographic medium (the claim that photography is mere mechanical reproduction and therefore not art), and its quick development into a form of mass entertainment, the cinema was not accepted as an art, at least initially. Classical film theorists therefore set out to show why and how the cinema is art. They did this, as Noël Carroll has demonstrated, by answering a series of questions about the cinema's unique properties, the role or value of these properties, and the stylistic techniques best suited to exploiting such properties.[2] This was because classical film theorists adhered, for the most part, to the doctrine of medium specificity, the view that in order for the cinema to be accepted as a legitimate art, it must be shown to possess valuable attributes of its own, ones that the other, preestablished arts do not have. Needless to say, theorists proposed different answers to these questions. This book is about one such answer, as well as its influence on contemporary film theory. According to this answer, the cinema's most significant property, one which the other arts do not possess (or at least do not possess to the same degree), is its ability to uncover features of reality invisible to human vision. The value of this property is that it can reveal the true nature of reality to viewers. And the techniques best suited to exploiting it, for reasons I will explore shortly, are those that least resemble human sight. I call this the revelationist answer.

The cinema's revelatory capacity is often mentioned in passing by classical film theorists when making arguments about the difference between cinema and the other arts. For example, Walter Benjamin claims that the cinema is helping to diminish if not destroy the "aura" traditionally possessed by works of art in part because it can reveal "entirely new structural formations of the subject" invisible to human vision. "Evidently a different nature opens itself to the camera than opens to the naked eye," he suggests.[3] The cinema's revelations in turn elicit a more analytical, "testing" attitude on the part of its viewers, he asserts, one that is antithetical to the reverence encouraged by auratic art.

There are, however, four classical film theorists who view the cinema's re-velatory power as its most important attribute and who devote a considerable amount of space to it in their writings rather than simply mention it in passing. These are Jean Epstein (1897–1953), Dziga Vertov (1896–1954), Béla Balázs (1884–1949), and Siegfried Kracauer (1889–1966). As Epstein put it in 1935, "cinematography renders perceptible through sight and sound individual beings we thought invisible and inaudible and divulges the reality of certain abstrac-tions."[4] And, according to Epstein, one of the abstractions revealed by the cinema is the fourth dimension of time, which human beings cannot see. As I show in the pages that follow, Vertov, Kracauer, and Balázs make similar arguments about the revelatory capacity of the cinema, although they differ considerably concern-ing the truths about reality it supposedly uncovers. Epstein and Vertov, who were filmmakers, also attempted to exploit this capacity in some of their films.

In advancing their claims about the cinema's revelatory power, these four theorists and filmmakers employ an analogy with considerable significance for their theories. They compare the cinema to microscopes and telescopes, argu-ing that, like them, it is capable of revealing truths about reality that are invis-ible in the sense that the human eye is incapable of seeing them unaided due to its limitations. It is this property, they seem to believe, that sets the cinema apart, because the other arts, with the exception of photography, lack the tech-nical means to reveal such truths. And while photography does possess some of these technical means, as an atemporal art its revelatory capacity is limited. For example, they frequently highlight the magnificatory power of the close-up, arguing that it can reveal various mobile features of reality that human vision is too weak to see, much like a microscope can reveal bacteria invisible to the naked eye. Balázs wrote:

> By means of the close-up the camera in the days of the silent film revealed also the hidden mainsprings of a life which we had thought we already knew so well. Blurred outlines are mostly the result of our insensitive short-sightedness and superficiality. We skim over the teeming substance of life. The camera has un-covered that cell-life of the vital issues in which all great events are ultimately conceived; for the greatest landslide is only the aggregate of the movements of single particles.[5]

They also often invoke the fact that the cinematic image is a photographic "trace," to use philosopher Gregory Currie's word, of what it depicts.[6] Al-though this property does not differentiate the cinema from photography, it does distinguish it from representational paintings, drawings, and sculptures.

For however reliable and accurate, hand-made representational art is a depiction of what its maker thinks or believes he or she is seeing (or has seen). A photograph, however, is independent of thoughts and beliefs in the following way: when working properly, a camera records, in the form of a photograph, what is in front of it, regardless of what the camera operator thinks or believes is in front of it. (Of course, whether and how photographs are created is not independent of thoughts and beliefs.) This independence from intentions has meant that many have viewed the cinema and photography as fundamentally different from the other arts, including Epstein, Vertov, Balázs, and Kracauer, although none of these theorists developed a theory of the photographic trace as others, such as André Bazin and, more recently, Kendall Walton have.

II

Nobody has investigated this answer to the question, what is cinema, although scholars have often noted its presence in classical film theory.[7] In the first half of this book, I undertake just such an investigation of the versions of it found in the writings, and where relevant the films, of Epstein, Vertov, Balázs, and Kracauer. Such a study is needed not only because their work constitutes an important but neglected tradition within the history of film theory, but because it has profound implications for film theory today.

The basic argument made by these four theorists and filmmakers is that certain cinematic techniques—the close-up, slow motion, time-lapse photography, editing—can reveal features of reality that are invisible in the sense that it is impossible for the human eye to see them without assistance. This claim is, in itself, perfectly reasonable; it is widely recognized that, in addition to being an art form, the cinema is a revelatory visual technology much like microscopes and telescopes. Indeed, it was at least in part invented by amateur and professional scientists, such as Marey, Muybridge, and Janssen, in order to discover and observe features of a diverse array of natural phenomena partially or wholly inaccessible to sight, such as the precise wing movements of birds or the exact leg positions of galloping horses. In the cinema's early years, before the industry-wide standardization of the narrative feature-length film in the mid-1910s, filmmakers often exploited the revelatory power of the cinema for entertainment purposes, making popular "scientific" films with "views of cholera germs, human sperm, fleas, plant pollination, and other subjects."[8] In his work of film theory of 1916, *The Photoplay: A Psychological Study,* Hugo Münsterberg describes this use of the cinema in his characteristically elegant fashion:

> After overcoming tremendous difficulties, the scientists succeeded in developing a microscope kinematography which multiplies the dimensions a hundred thousand times. We may see on the screen the fight of the bacteria with the microscopically small blood corpuscles in the blood stream of a diseased animal. Yes, by the miracles of the camera we may trace the life of nature even in forms which no human observation really finds in the outer world.[9]

However, in conjunction with this uncontroversial claim, the work of Epstein, Vertov, Balázs, and Kracauer contains another, more mysterious feature: all four invest the cinema's revelatory capacity with considerable significance, arguing that revelation is its most important property. There is, of course, good reason to be happy about the existence of any visual technology that can uncover features of reality inaccessible to human vision. Such technologies extend our perceptual and cognitive access to the natural universe around us, thereby enabling us to better explain, predict, and control it and, in turn, improve our well-being. For example, observing through a microscope the properties of a pathogenic bacterium helps us understand how the microbe infects the human body and find ways to protect ourselves from it, thereby controlling or eradicating whatever disease it causes.

But these four theorists and filmmakers go well beyond mere happiness about the existence of the cinema. And they do not spend much time focusing on the way it improves our ability to explain, predict, and control the natural universe. Instead, to varying degrees in their writings, they express near-religious extremes of euphoria about its revelatory capacity. And they conceive of it as an awesome, even miraculous power that, rather than extending the power of the human eye, escapes its limitations and thereby has the potential to bring about a fundamental change for the better in human existence.

For example, in the following passage, Epstein places the film within a lineage of inventions that, by virtue of their differences from the human body, escapes its limitations:

> The essence of living is surpassing oneself. Man had to do more than walk; he invented the wheel, which is something other than the leg. He had to do more than swim; hence the propeller is something other than the flagellum. And needing to do more than see, man augmented the microscopic and telescopic apparatuses with the cinematic apparatus, creating something other than the eye. . . . once [the cinema] addresses all of the senses, each will be able to surpass its physiological limitations.[10]

Confident in the superhuman power of its revelatory capacity, Epstein draws the following conclusion about the cinema's potential to alter human life for the better: "Now we are approaching the promised land, a place of great wonders. . . . This is why some of us have entrusted to [cinema] our highest hopes.[11]

Epstein's sense of the cinema's freedom from human perceptual limitations and its potential to change the world for the better is everywhere evident in Vertov's film theory:

> I am kino-eye, I am a mechanical eye. I, a machine, show you the world as only I can see it. Now and forever, I free myself from human immobility, I am in constant motion, I draw near, then away from objects, I crawl under, I climb onto them. I move apace with the muzzle of a galloping horse, I plunge full speed into a crowd, I outstrip running soldiers, I fall on my back, I ascend with an airplane, I plunge and soar together with plunging and soaring bodies.[12]

Rather than arguing that the cinema extends the power of the human eye, Vertov claims that, before the invention of the cinema, people couldn't see at all, at least as far as social reality is concerned. As we shall discover, Vertov argues that the cinema allows people to see the true nature of social reality for the first time, thereby escaping their condition of blindness toward it: "The eyes of children and adults, the educated as well as the uneducated, are opening, as it were, for the first time. Millions of workers, having recovered their sight."[13]

Balázs, meanwhile, claims that the cinema has brought about the evolution of new perceptual and cognitive abilities in human beings: "The birth of film art led not only to the creation of new works of art but to the emergence of new human faculties with which to perceive and understand this new art." He declares that it is the task of his film theory to "investigate and outline that sphere of the development of human sensibility which developed in mutual interaction with the evolution of the art of the film."[14] Because it has led to the evolution of new perceptual and cognitive abilities, Balázs, like Epstein and Vertov, pronounces the invention of the cinema to be an epochal transformation for the better in human existence.

> The evolution of the human capacity for understanding which was brought about by the art of the film, opened a new chapter in the history of human culture. . . . We were witnesses not only of the development of a new art but of the development of a new sensibility, a new understanding, a new culture in its public. . . . WE HAVE LEARNED TO SEE.[15]

Finally, in 1960 Kracauer made a claim similar to Vertov's, although for different reasons. According to Kracauer, it is physical rather than social reality to which humans were blind before the invention of the cinema, because it had been "persistently veiled by ideologies" prior to modernity, and then again by "the habit of abstract thinking we have acquired under the reign of science and technology"[16] in modernity.

> Film renders visible what we did not, or perhaps even could not, see before its advent. It effectively assists us in discovering the material world with its psychophysical correspondences. We literally redeem this world from its dormant state, its state of virtual nonexistence, by endeavoring to experience it through the camera.[17]

As we shall see, Kracauer thinks that the cinema enables people to escape the condition of blindness toward physical reality, and as a result he also believes that it can transform life for the better by helping people "escape from [the] spiritual nakedness" of modernity.[18]

Admittedly, it is typical for people to get excited about new technologies until they become accustomed to them—to wit, the irrational exuberance about digital technologies of the last decade of the twentieth century. Film was certainly no exception. As historians of early cinema have shown, its invention was greeted with a great deal of wonder, and its first viewers paid money primarily to witness the technological marvel of a moving photographic image.

However, Epstein, Vertov, Balázs, and Kracauer began writing about the cinema and making films at least twenty years after its first appearance, long after it had ceased to be a technological novelty. Furthermore, visual technologies capable of revealing features of reality inaccessible to the naked human eye, such as microscopes and telescopes, had been around for a lot longer than film. Why, then, did these theorists and filmmakers view the cinema's revelatory power as so important?

They held this view, I argue here, because of their doubts about human vision—their conviction that our sense of sight fails to give us genuine knowledge of reality.[19] Due to this visual skepticism, they desired to escape the human eye's limitations in order to see reality as it really is, not as it appears to our flawed visual faculty.[20] And they believed that the cinema's revelatory capacity, in combination with the fact that it is a machine and therefore partially free of human intentions, makes it something other than the eye and affords just such an escape. Furthermore, because the cinema is not only a technology like a microscope or telescope, but an art and a mass art at that, they hoped that its revelatory power would affect humanity in general by opening the eyes of the masses to the true nature of reality. For them, the cinema had the potential to be an art of mass enlightenment, and this is why they held its revelatory power in such high regard. In the first chapter of this book, I examine in detail the particular criticisms of human vision made by these theorists and filmmakers and the various truths about reality that each believed the cinema could reveal. Their work, like so much in modern culture, divides into two branches. The first, the naturalist branch, exemplified by Epstein and Vertov, argues that the human eye fails to see the true nature of reality due to innate handicaps. The second, the culturalist branch, typified by Balázs and Kracauer, claims that it is cultural forces at work in modernity that prevent people from seeing reality or aspects of it.

III

Much excellent scholarship has already been published on the work of these theorists and filmmakers. David Bordwell, Stuart Liebman, and Richard Abel have shed light on Epstein's difficult theory and practice by interpreting it within the context of French film theories, art history, and early twentieth-century French philosophy, as have several recent volumes in French.[21] Joseph Zsuffa, Sabine Hake, and Hanno Loewy have done the same with Balázs's theory in the German context.[22] Annette Michelson and Vlada Petric have illuminated Vertov's writings and films by situating them within the context of debates among Soviet modernists about the role of art in the construction of a socialist society in the 1920s, and a new wave of Vertov scholarship by Yuri Tsivian, John MacKay, and others is filling in gaps in our knowledge of the historical landscape in which Vertov worked.[23] Finally, there is now a veritable industry of interpretation on how Kracauer's early film theory constitutes a response to modernity in the Weimar Republic (although much less attention has been devoted to his later *Theory of Film*, 1960).[24]

In what follows, I occasionally borrow from the insights of these scholars while taking a different approach. Instead of investigating these four theorists and filmmakers individually, as others have done, I examine them together, showing how they share a distrust of human vision and a concomitant desire to escape the limitations of human seeing by way of the revelatory power of the cinema. Nobody has examined the influence of skepticism about sight on film, but it is fundamental, at least in the case of these theorists and filmmakers. The considerable value Epstein, Vertov, Balázs, and Kracauer attach to the cinema's revelatory capacity, and their attendant euphoria about it, can only be understood within the context of their distrust of human vision, and considering them together throws this distrust into sharp relief.

Additionally, and more important, their work constitutes a distinct tradition within the history of the cinema, one that has been overlooked and which this book seeks to bring to light. This tradition differs in significant ways from the cinema's two major traditions, modernism and realism, as can be demonstrated by examining how its adherents answer the question, what is cinema?

It is commonly assumed that two answers to this question have dominated film theory and filmmaking since they began. The first answer is that the cinema's most significant artistic property is "its capacity to manipulate reality, that is, to rearrange and thereby reconstitute the profilmic event (the event that transpires in front of the camera)."[25] This answer is identified as modernist because it is predicated on conceptions of art prevalent in modernism, particularly antimimetic conceptions.

A famous example of this modernist, antimimetic answer is provided by Rudolf Arnheim in his *Film as Art,* first published in 1933. According to Arnheim, if a filmmaker wishes to create a work of art, he cannot merely mechanically record and thereby reproduce what is in front of the camera. Rather, he must in some way transform it using unique cinematic techniques.

> The film producer himself is influenced by the strong resemblance of his photographic material to reality. As distinguished from the tools of the sculptor and the painter, which by themselves produce nothing resembling nature, the camera starts to turn and a likeness of the real world results mechanically. There is serious danger that the film maker will rest content with such shapeless reproduction. In order that the film artist may create a work of art it is important that he consciously stress the peculiarities of his medium.[26]

Other modernist film theorists such as Hugo Münsterberg, Soviet montage filmmakers of the 1920s such as Lev Kuleshov and Sergei Eisenstein, and most of the French Impressionist filmmakers of the 1920s, such as Germaine Dulac, concur that the cinema's most important feature is its capacity to manipulate reality.

The second of the historically dominant answers to the question, what is cinema, is that the cinema's most significant artistic property is its capacity to reproduce, rather than manipulate, reality. The most famous exponent of this theory is probably André Bazin. Bazin, who grew to maturity in the 1930s when realism renewed its influence on Western artists and intellectuals, offers a number of arguments in his writings for why this is so. One focuses on the fact that photographs mechanically record reality. When exposed, the chemicals on the surface of a photograph automatically register the light bouncing off whatever the camera is pointing toward. According to Bazin, a photograph therefore "shares, by virtue of the very process of its becoming, the being of the model of which it is the reproduction; it *is* the model."[27] This means that photographs allow humans to "re-present" reality for the first time in history.

> This production by automatic means has radically affected our psychology of the image. The objective nature of photography confers on it a quality of credibility absent from all other picture-making. In spite of any objections our critical spirit may offer, we are forced to accept as real the existence of the object reproduced, actually *re*-presented, set before us, that is to say, in time and space. Photography enjoys a certain advantage in virtue of this transference of reality from the thing to its reproduction.[28]

Cinema goes one step further in re-presenting reality than does still photography, Bazin argues, because "for the first time, the image of things is likewise the image of their duration, change mummified as it were."[29]

While I do not dispute that these two answers—the modernist and the realist—to the question, what is cinema, are influential even to this day, there are others, including the one that is the subject of this book—namely, that the cinema's most significant feature is its capacity to reveal truths about reality invisible to the naked human eye. This revelationist answer constitutes a distinct alternative to the historically dominant ones of modernism and realism. Like the realist answer, it views the cinema's ability to mechanically record and reproduce reality as a valuable one, rather than denigrating it, as do modernists such as Arnheim. The theorists and filmmakers I examine in the first two chapters of this book constantly laud the cinema's capacity to reproduce reality as it really is, and they attribute its ability to do so, in part, to its mechanical, photographic nature.

However, they distrust human vision, and it is this skepticism that sets them apart from realists such as Bazin, because a common feature of realism is a belief in the capacity of the naked human eye to see reality. Linda Nochlin, in her seminal work on realism, cites the writings of Edgar Degas as an example of this faith in vision in nineteenth-century realism: "In his notebooks, Degas reiterated in both words and sketches his passion for concrete, direct observation and notation of ordinary, everyday experience."[30] In Bazin's writings, we often encounter a similar faith in human vision along with the view that certain films are realist art works because they imitate features of human sight. In an article on the filmmaker William Wyler, for example, Bazin argues that "'realism' consists not only of showing us a corpse, but also of showing it to us under conditions that re-create certain physiological or mental givens of natural perception."[31] And Bazin celebrates directors such as Wyler and Jean Renoir for their use of stylistic techniques such as the long take that, supposedly, better imitate the "givens of natural perception" than editing.

For Epstein, Vertov, Balázs, and Kracauer, human vision does not give us genuine knowledge of reality. Hence, they view those stylistic techniques that least resemble human sight as most likely to reproduce it. As Vertov put it:

> Until now many a cameraman has been criticized for having filmed a running horse moving with unnatural slowness on the screen (rapid cranking of the camera)—or for the opposite, a tractor plowing a field too swiftly (slow cranking of the camera), and the like.
>
> These are chance occurrences, of course, but we are preparing a system, a deliberate system of such occurrences, a system of seeming irregularities to investigate and organize phenomena.
>
> Until now, we have violated the movie camera and forced it to copy the work of our eye. And the better the copy, the better the shooting was thought to be. Starting today we are liberating the camera and making it work in the opposite direction—away from copying.[32]

The techniques of slow and fast motion mentioned by Vertov at the beginning of this passage, along with reverse motion, extreme close-ups or long shots, and editing are also celebrated by modernists such as Arnheim for their antimimetic properties. But unlike modernists, those in the revelationist tradition do not view these techniques as incompatible with reproducing reality. Rather, they celebrate them, along with the cinema's capacity to mechanically record reality, because they supposedly better enable filmmakers to reproduce reality as it is and not as it appears to humans with their flawed sense of sight.

Because the revelationist answer to the question, what is cinema, shares features with both the modernist and realist answers, there has been some debate about how to categorize the work of the theorists and filmmakers who propose it. Dudley Andrew's book *The Major Film Theories,* for example, has been criticized by Sabine Hake for placing Balázs with Arnheim in the "formative" or modernist tradition, and Kracauer in the realist; Theodor Adorno famously called Kracauer a "curious realist" because his work does not fit the usual definition of realism.[33] However, Balázs, Kracauer, Epstein, and Vertov belong in neither camp. Rather, they propose an answer to the question that, while sharing features with them, is distinct from both the realist and modernist answers.

IV

This book also differs from the work of other scholars in that it is primarily a work of theory, not history. My goal is not only to better understand the theories that are its subject, but to advance arguments about them and offer a critique of the revelationist tradition.

Like much film theory, the writings of Epstein, Vertov, Balázs, and Kracauer are rife with the sort of logical and empirical errors that philosophers and theorists of film have exposed and criticized in recent years, such as adherence to the doctrine of medium specificity.[34] Instead of retreading ground already covered so well, I focus on a mistake that has not been addressed by others. Theorists and filmmakers in the revelationist tradition, I demonstrate in chapter 2, are only able to make their arguments about the limitations of human vision and the revelatory power of the cinema by misusing perceptual and related concepts. This takes a particular form in their writings. If we look closely at the truths about reality that, according to them, are revealed by the cinema, we find that in many cases they turn out to differ considerably from the sort of empirical phenomena (such as a distant planet, the particulate structure of an object, or microbes) that are normally discovered and observed using visual technologies. In some cases, they are not the kinds of things that the naked human eye fails to see because it is not powerful enough. Instead, they are things that it is logically—not empirically—impossible for people to see, with or without the aid of a visual instrument. As the philosopher Ludwig Wittgenstein pointed out, not being able to, for example, see sounds is not an empirical failing on the part of human perception.[35] It is not because eyes are too weak that they cannot see a sound. Rather, seeing a sound is logically excluded by the meaning of the concepts of sight and sound. It makes no sense to say, "I couldn't see that sound—it was too far away"; one can only fail to see what it makes sense to be able to see in the first place, such as a distant planet. To state that a sound cannot be seen is to say something about the meaning of the concepts of sight and sound, to express a rule of logical grammar about their use. It is not to claim that eyes fail to see sounds because they are not strong enough.

Similarly, the truths about reality revealed by the cinema in the theories I am examining often logically exclude the possibility of being seen, with or without the aid of a visual technology. The past and the future, for example, are not things that, logically speaking, it is possible for people to see, I argue in chapter 2. The human eye does not fail to see beyond the present because it is too weak. Yet Epstein conceives of the fourth dimension of time as if it were an empirical phenomenon that the naked eye is not powerful enough to see but that can be revealed by the cinema in the same way that the position of a planet too distant for the eye to see can be revealed by a telescope. For Vertov, as Annette Michelson has demonstrated, it is the true "relations of workers with each other," as theorized by Marxist-Leninism, that are made visible by the cinema.[36] Again, such relations are not the sort of thing, logically speaking, that can be seen, as I demonstrate in chapter 2. Yet, Vertov describes social relations between workers as if they were an empirical phenomenon that vision is not powerful enough to see but that can be observed with the aid of the cinema, much like the particulate structure of an object can be observed with the aid of a microscope.

The truths about reality uncovered by the cinema in Balázs's and Kracauer's theories also bear little resemblance to the phenomena that it is logically possible to observe using visual technologies, as we will also see in chapter 2. For example, in Balázs's theory, one such truth is an individual's inner, mental life. Yet the mind (as opposed to the brain) is not an empirical feature of reality that the naked human eye fails to see because it is not powerful enough. The flesh and bone of the skull do not prevent thoughts and feelings from being seen in the same way that they keep the brain from being seen; we do not fail to see what a person is feeling because we cannot open up her skull. Rather, we fail to see that a person is feeling sad, or thinking hard, if we are not observant enough, or if the person is hiding these things from us, not because our visual faculty is too weak to see thoughts and feelings and we need an X-ray or some other visual technology in order to see them, as we do, say, Broca's area.

In other instances, paradoxically enough, the opposite is true. Some of these theorists argue that the cinema reveals things that it is logically and empirically possible for people to see without the aid of a visual technology. For example, when arguing that one of the features of reality laid bare by the cinema is the inner, mental life of human beings, Balázs claims that a close-up can reveal the true thoughts and feelings in a liar's face, and he cites as an example a scene from an Eisenstein film (presumably *The Battleship Potemkin*) in which a priest appears, at first, "like the sublime image of a saint" (fig. I.1):

> But then the camera gives an isolated big close-up of one eye; and a cunningly watchful furtive glance slinks out from under his beautiful silky eyelashes like an ugly caterpillar out of a delicate flower. Then the handsome priest turns his head and a close-up shows the back of his head and the lobe of his ear from behind. And we see the ruthless, vicious selfishness of a coarse peasant expressed in them.[37]

By means of a close-up, the camera in this scene, according to Balázs, reveals a "different, more profound truth" about the priest: the true "selfishness" concealed beneath his sublime visage (fig. I.2). But Balázs does not acknowledge that, while the close-up may be drawing the viewer's attention to details of the priest's appearance that he or she might not have noticed otherwise, it certainly is not revealing anything that people cannot see without assistance. A "cunning glance" can be observed without the aid of a visual technology, just as "selfishness" can be seen in a person's face. Yet Balázs describes these and related details as empirical features of reality that, like microbes, need to be revealed by the cinema because the human eye is unable to see them. Kracauer does the same. In cataloguing the cinema's "revealing functions," he suggests

Figure I.1. According to Balázs, the priest at first appears "sublime" in *The Battleship Potemkin* (Sergei Eisenstein, 1925).

14 DOUBTING VISION

that "transient" phenomena, such as "the manes of . . . galloping horses," are a good example of the sort of thing "normally unseen" by people that the cinema reveals.[38] However, like Balázs, Kracauer seems to forget that, while a film might draw a viewer's attention via a close-up or some other technique to details of a galloping horse that he or she might not have noticed otherwise, such as its mane, it certainly is not revealing anything that people cannot see unassisted.

Thus, there is what the philosopher Gilbert Ryle called a category mistake running rampant in the revelationist tradition, which this book seeks to expose and diagnose. Just as, according to Ryle, the "official doctrine" of the mind perpetuated by Descartes "represents the facts of mental life as if they belonged to one logical type or category (or range of types or categories), when they actually belong to another,"[39] so these theorists, in making their arguments about the limitations of human vision, confuse things that the eye is too weak to see but that can be revealed by a visual technology with things that it is logically impossible for people to see with or without the help of a visual technology and things that it is logically and empirically possible for humans to see unaided.

It might be thought that exposing this category mistake can only be of historical interest now because film theory has advanced well beyond the revelationist tradition since the 1960s. Due to the linguistic and cultural turn that occurred in the Anglo-American arts and humanities in the 1960s, film theorists over the last four decades have tended to embrace the view that human subjectivity is inescapable. Hence, they have, on the whole, abandoned the argument that the cinema escapes the eye's limitations by revealing truths about reality that it cannot see. Although this has indeed happened, it does not mean that the revelationist tradition fell into obsolescence in the 1960s. In fact, as I show in chapter 3, its conception of the cinema as a revelatory artistic medium, and the distrust of human vision upon which this conception is founded, have been renewed by semiotic-psychoanalytical film theorists, Stanley Cavell, proponents of the so-called modernity thesis, and Gilles Deleuze. Contemporary film theorists still tend to view human seeing as limited, and the cinema as capable of revealing truths that human beings cannot see. And, like their pre-

Figure I.2. A close-up of the priest in *The Battleship Potemkin* reveals his true "selfishness."

decessors in the revelationist tradition, they advance their arguments about the failings of human vision and the cinema's revelatory power at the price of misusing perceptual and related concepts. One of the reasons I am so concerned to criticize the revelationist tradition is that it has bequeathed to the study of film a careless attitude toward the meanings of such concepts that is still very much with us. Indeed, we will find in the case of Deleuze's theory, the most contemporary film theory I examine, repetitions of some of the same mistakes made by Epstein and Vertov. In this respect at least, the break between classical and contemporary film theory is more apparent than real.

This book therefore might seem to be a work of destructive criticism, and in some ways it is. Throughout, I criticize the arguments about the limitations of human sight that have constituted one of the foundations of film theory since the 1920s by showing that theorists and filmmakers routinely misuse perceptual concepts in making these arguments. And in chapter 4, I briefly point to some philosophical reasons why it is wrong to distrust human vision even though it is fallible. Visual skepticism, I conclude, is probably not a solid foundation on which to build theories of film. However, this book also has constructive goals. First, I seek to understand why it is that theorists and filmmakers have succumbed to skepticism about sight. This can be explained, I argue in chapter 4, by the fact that such skepticism provides a powerful rationale for the purpose of cinematic art, thereby fulfilling the central task of classical film theory: to prove that the cinema is an art. Second, having shown throughout in what ways the cinema is not a revelatory art, in chapter 4 I clarify some legitimate senses in which it is. The cinema certainly can "reveal truths about reality" in ways the other arts cannot. But, as we shall see, it does not do so, at least primarily, in the sense meant by theorists and filmmakers in the revelationist tradition. They assumed incorrectly that the revelation of inaccessible natural phenomena by visual technologies is the paradigm of cinematic revelation in general, which is one source of the theoretical problems I expose in this book. Once we rid ourselves of this misleading assumption and attain a grasp of other senses in which the cinema is a revelatory art, we can do justice to their claim that it allows us "to see more and better" than the other arts by reconstructing it in a more plausible form. Indeed, we can better appreciate their genuine insights into the revelatory powers of the cinema and the ways cinema differs from the other arts as they are customarily practiced.[40]

I'd like to say a word or two about the philosophical tradition I draw on to criticize film-theoretical claims about the limitations of human vision. This is the tradition of analytical philosophy pioneered by Wittgenstein and Ryle in the mid-twentieth century and further developed by many other philosophers, which consists primarily of the method, on display throughout this book, of clarifying the meanings of concepts and their interconnections to show where and how theorists transgress the bounds of sense.[41] This is not a tradition that has been used much in the study of film. Indeed, most Anglo-American scholars of the arts are unfamiliar with it. I therefore need to say a little about it and why I turn to it.[42] (Those readers already knowledgeable about this tradition may want to skip ahead to the final three paragraphs of this introduction.)

According to Wittgenstein, the subject matter, questions, problems, and solutions of philosophy are fundamentally different from those of empirical disciplines because they are not empirical in nature. While the natural sciences, for example, aim to explain empirical phenomena, philosophy is concerned exclusively with something that antecedes and is separable from empirical inquiry, namely, questions of sense and meaning. The basic distinction at stake here can be illustrated, provisionally, by invoking a simple, canonical example. The sentence "a bachelor cannot be married" seems to state a general proposition about bachelors that is akin to a general empirical proposition like "all cows eat grass." However, it does not state a general fact, one that can be proven or disproven by empirical research in the way that the claim "all cows eat grass" can be. Rather, the "cannot" of the first sentence is logical, not empirical. Someone who understands the English language knows in advance of any empirical investigation that a bachelor cannot be married, that empirical research will never turn up a married bachelor. And he knows this because it is part of the logic of the word "bachelor," part of its sense or meaning that, if one says that someone is a bachelor, he cannot also be married. The sentence in question exhibits this aspect of the meaning of the word "bachelor" by specifying a necessary condition of its use, rather than by making an empirical claim about the world.

Wittgenstein argued that genuine philosophy is concerned purely with the type of subject matter this sentence exhibits, with what can be known about language in advance of any empirical research, namely, the sense or meaning of the words, expressions, and sentences it contains. Philosophy, he thought, has nothing of an empirical nature to discover about language or anything else. As he put it in the *Philosophical Investigations:*

> And we may not advance any kind of theory. There must not be anything hypothetical in our considerations. We must do away with all *explanation,* and description alone must take its place. And this description gets its light, that is to say its purpose, from the philosophical problems. These are, of course, not empirical problems; they are solved, rather, by looking into the workings of our language, and that in such a way as to make us recognize those workings: *in despite of* an urge to misunderstand them. These problems are solved, not by giving new information.[43]

Philosophy is concerned with "the workings of our language," with what is already in place, not something unknown. The questions it asks are about sense and meaning, not what is true and false; its problems result from the transgression of sense into nonsense, not from a deficit of empirical information; and its solutions consist of showing when and how such transgressions take place, not discovering new facts.[44]

To those unfamiliar with Wittgenstein's work and the tradition of philosophy he helped spawn, this might seem like a trivial conception of philosophy. Gone, for instance, is the grand enterprise of theory building in the image of science or the construction of speculative systems found in so much philosophy. In their place is the apparently mundane activity of describing how linguistic expressions are used in practice. However, even if one does not accept Wittgenstein's claim that philosophy should be concerned exclusively with questions of meaning, when one realizes the consequences of failures to grasp the correct use of language, the importance of the philosopher's task as articulated by Wittgenstein becomes all too clear. For although as language users we come to master the meanings of the expressions in our language and employ them correctly with ease, we typically lack the ability to articulate the rules governing their use, just as we follow rules when we speak and write (such as the rules that govern the position of adjectives before nouns), yet we typically lack the ability to state in a propositional form what these rules are (unless we have been taught how to do so). While as ordinary language users we do not normally need to be able to clarify the logic of our language, there are contexts in which this inability can have major ramifications—for example, when theorizing about the mind or the senses, or employing mental and perceptual concepts in studying the arts. Without this ability, we can easily violate the meanings of such concepts and stray beyond the bounds of sense into nonsense. "A main source of our failure to understand is that we do not *command a clear view* of the use of our words—Our grammar is lacking in this sort of perspicuity" (PI §122; emphasis in the original).

The philosopher Anthony Kenny provides a simple example of how we can stray beyond the bounds of sense into nonsense due to a failure to clarify the logic of our language: the confusion between abilities and the agents of these abilities (which Kenny calls "vehicles"). A car in motion, for example, has the ability to stop, and the brake mechanism makes this ability possible. Similarly, human beings and other creatures have the ability to see, and the eye, as well as certain parts of the brain, makes this ability possible. There is a category difference between the two. An agent of ability is a concrete, space-occupying entity, something that can be weighed and measured, whereas an ability has neither length, breadth, width, or location. It is identified instead through its exercise in appropriate circumstances by its possessor. Yet, as Kenny warns, there is a temptation to "hypostatize" abilities, "to treat them as if they were substances or parts or ingredients of their substances."[45] An example would be to think of the ability (or disposition) to act virtuously as a substance present in a virtuous person, something which can be discovered and measured in the same way that the alcohol present in the bloodstream of an intoxicated person can. This may seem like an obvious category difference that no sane person would fail to heed. Yet, as Kenny and other philosophers have pointed out, the distinction between ability and agent is routinely lost by those contemporary philosophers and neuroscientists who claim that the mind is the brain. The brain, as the agent of the mind, is a physical object, while the mind is not, because it is made up of capacities such as the ability to learn a language. Whole philosophical systems and research programs have been built on the confusion between the two. (In chapter 3 we will discover that at least one contemporary film theorist, Deleuze, is not immune from the confusion between ability and agent.)

I turn to this philosophical tradition because it provides compelling answers to questions about the meanings of perceptual and related concepts. Without a solid grasp of their meanings, it is easy to misuse these concepts and thereby participate in conceptual confusion. As this book shows, such confusion is rife in the writings of theorists in the revelationist tradition, and it remains rife in the writings of their descendants. Although film theorists routinely make empirical claims about what we see when watching films, few have stopped to ask what it makes sense to say that we can see when doing so. Indeed, few have asked what "seeing" means. The later philosophy of Wittgenstein in particular provides answers to these questions in its careful examination of how perceptual concepts are customarily used in practice.[46]

It might be objected that film theorists do not use perceptual concepts in an ordinary fashion, and therefore that an investigation into how they are normally employed in the way Wittgenstein did has little relevance to film theory. Instead, it could be argued, film theorists use perceptual concepts in a technical or metaphorical sense, as is common in science and the arts. This is an objection often used to defend theory against conceptual analysis and critique.[47] However, one of the reasons I bring analytical philosophy to bear on the revelationist tradition is that revelationists do not clarify precisely in what way they are using perceptual concepts. By elucidating how we customarily use these concepts, at the very least we can tell whether their use by film theorists conforms to our ordinary one, and, if it does not, we can conclude that their claims do not apply to perception as we normally conceive it. More important, all the evidence suggests that these theorists do believe that their arguments are of relevance to perception as normally understood, for if they did not, they would not draw the conclusions that they do. Nor would they attach so much importance to the cinema. If it was vision in some secondary sense that their arguments applied to, they would not claim that the cinema is a revolutionary artistic medium because it reveals reality as it really is and not as it appears to our flawed sense of sight for the simple reason that their arguments would not be about sight in the literal, ordinary sense. For instance, when Epstein, following Henri Bergson, blames the eye for "Man's physiological inability to master the notion of space-time and to escape this atemporal section of the world, which we call the present and of which we are almost exclusively conscious,"[48] it must be normal, literal perception that he is speaking of; otherwise he would not also claim that the cinema, in making "another perspective of matter evident, that of time,"[49] is forcing us to abandon the "fixed, discrete notions" of reality typical of both "philosophy" and our "common-sense" view of the world.

> No more than twenty years have been spent on tentative research, and we can already measure the significance of the change that the cinema—in its expression of the external and internal movement of all beings—has brought to bear on our thinking. Even now, we correct ourselves according to a reality where time never stops, where values only exist so long as they vary, where nothing exists except in becoming, where a phenomenon without velocity is inconceivable.[50]

If it was only vision in some technical or metaphorical sense that Epstein's arguments about the failures of human sight applied to, he would not make euphoric claims like the one above about the transformative impact of the cinema on human life, because he would not be arguing that the human eye is literally incapable of escaping "this atemporal section of the world," or that the cinema is literally capable of doing so.

But even if readers are not swayed by the specific criticisms I make of the revelationist tradition and its descendants, I hope that at the very least this book will draw attention to the importance of questions about sense and meaning. Scholars of film, like scholars of the arts more generally, devote perilously little time to clarifying the meanings of the concepts they use, a problem which this book aims to begin rectifying. I also hope this book will bring to light the revelationist tradition and its contemporary influence. Classical film theory was a much richer, more complex and more varied enterprise than the argument between modernists and realists about the nature of cinematic art that it is often reduced to, and it continues to influence contemporary film theory to a greater extent than is often realized. Epstein, Vertov, Balázs, and Kracauer each made imaginative but flawed contributions to this enterprise by proposing original versions of the revelationist claim that the cinema uncovers truths about reality that cannot be seen with the naked human eye, and their arguments and assumptions are influential to this day.

1

The Revelationist Tradition

Exegesis

I

Not all of Jean Epstein's film theory is informed by a distrust of human vision. In one of his first major articles on film, published in 1921, he argues that sight is our most advanced perceptual and cognitive faculty, and praises the cinema for being primarily a visual art.

> Although sight is already recognized by everyone as the most developed sense, and even though the viewpoint of our intellect and our mores is visual, there has nevertheless never been an emotive process so homogeneously, so exclusively optical as the cinema. Truly, the cinema creates *a particular system of consciousness limited to a single sense.*[1]

According to Epstein, because of the size of the screen onto which films are projected as well as stylistic techniques such as the close-up, the cinema is able to capture and occupy the viewer's attention through his or her eyes alone, relegating information from the other senses to a minor or nonexistent role.[2] "The cinematic feeling is therefore particularly intense," he concludes, because it is free of supposedly inferior perceptual and cognitive capacities such as hearing.[3]

Elsewhere in his writings, however, Epstein is less enamored of human vision, especially when he turns his attention away from the cinema's emotional effects toward its capacity to reveal truths about reality invisible to the naked eye. One of these truths, on which he focuses throughout his writings, is mobility. Epstein, like many artists and intellectuals of his generation, was influenced by the philosopher Henri Bergson, and, according to Bergson's metaphysics, reality is an indivisible, continuous whole that both endures and changes unpredictably. This is because everything is connected to, and constantly interacting with, everything else throughout time and space. One consequence of this condition is that matter is mobile. As Bergson puts it in *Matter and Memory*, "Matter thus resolves itself into numberless vibrations, all linked together in uninterrupted continuity, all bound up with each other, and traveling in every direction like shivers through an immense body."[4] Meanwhile, human sight cannot perceive the mobility of reality because, for reasons I explore in a moment, for Bergson "to perceive means to immobilize."[5] According to Epstein, the cinema can reveal this mobility: "Such also is the clairvoyance of cinematography which represents [the] world in its overall, continuous mobility. Faithful to the etymology of its name, it discovers movement where our eye sees nothing but stasis."[6] The close-up is one of the techniques that enables the cinema to do so due to its magnificatory power. When the face is filmed in close-up, for example:

> Muscular preambles ripple beneath the skin. Shadows shift, tremble, hesitate. Something is being decided. A breeze of emotion underlines the mouth with clouds. The orography of the face vacillates. Seismic shocks begin. Capillary wrinkles try to split the fault. A wave carries them away. Crescendo. A muscle bridles. The lip is laced with tics like a theater curtain. Everything is movement, imbalance, crisis.[7]

Epstein also argues that the cinema is more reliable than human vision because it is a machine.

> My eye presents me with an idea of a form; the film stock also contains an idea of a form, an idea established independently of my awareness, an idea without awareness, a latent, secret but marvelous idea. . . . Because this unexpected discovery of a subject that is an object without conscience—without hesitation or scruples, that is, devoid of venality, indulgence, or possible error, an entirely honest artist, exclusively an artist, the model artist—must be put to use.[8]

Epstein claims that the revelation of mobility by the cinema shows that human sight is deeply flawed. In demonstrating that reality is mobile, "an amazing animism is restored to the world [by the cinema]. We know now, once we've seen it, that we are surrounded by inhuman living things."[9] This animistic, mobile reality, Epstein asserts, is fundamentally at odds with the static one that people see and take for granted. "These [cinematic] experiments contradict and throw into confusion the sense of order which we have established at great cost in our conception of the universe. . . . Not without some anxiety, man finds himself before that chaos which he has covered up, denied, forgotten, or thought was tamed. Cinematography apprises him of a monster."[10] In fact, so different is the animistic, mobile reality revealed by the cinema from the one people normally see and assume to exist that Epstein often employs primitivist similes and metaphors to describe its inhuman strangeness:

> Those lives [the cinema] creates . . . have little in common with human life. These lives are like the life in charms and amulets, the ominous, tabooed objects of certain primitive religions. If we wish to understand how an animal, a plant, or a stone can inspire respect, fear, or horror, those three most sacred sentiments, I think we must watch them on the screen, living their mysterious, silent lives, alien to the human sensibility.[11]

Given the wide gap in Epstein's theory between reality as it really is and the way it appears to human vision, it is not surprising that he argues that the cinema's revelatory capacity escapes the eye's limitations rather than extending its power, as we saw in his claim that the cinema is "something other than the eye."[12]

One of the sources of Epstein's belief that the naked human eye is unable to see the true nature of reality is his knowledge of modern science. Scientists and philosophers since Galileo have argued that, while the world appears to humans to be multicolored, noisy, many-scented, and hot or cold, in reality there is only the rapid movement of colorless, noiseless, scentless particles, of waves of air or electro-magnetic radiation. This gap between appearance and reality has typically been explained by the doctrine of "secondary qualities," which argues that qualities such as color, taste, sound, and smell are not properties of objects, as they seem to be to humans. Rather, they are produced in us by the action of objects on our sense organs and are, at least in part, subjective in origin. For many modern philosophers and scientists, human perceptual organs therefore fail to perceive reality as it really is. As Alfred Whitehead famously put it in *Science and the Modern World*:

> Bodies are perceived as with qualities which in reality do not belong to them, qualities which in fact are purely the offspring of the mind. Thus nature gets credit which should in truth be reserved for ourselves; the rose for its scent; the nightingale for his song; and the sun for his radiance. The poets are entirely mistaken. They should address their lyrics to themselves, and should turn them into odes of self-congratulation on the excellency of the human mind. Nature is a dull affair, soundless, scentless, colourless; merely the hurrying of material, endlessly, meaninglessly.[13]

Epstein is clearly aware of the doctrine of secondary qualities, which he appeals to in this passage from 1921: "The senses, of course, present us only with symbols of reality: uniform, proportionate, elective metaphors. And symbols not of matter, which therefore does not exist, but of energy; that is, of something which in itself seems not to be, except in its effects as they affect us. We say 'red,' 'soprano,' 'sweet,' 'cypress,' when there are only velocities, movements, vibrations."[14] In contrast, the cinema, he argues, is able to reveal the reality hidden by secondary qualities: the "waves invisible to us, and the screen's creative passion [which] contains what no other has ever had before; its proper share of ultraviolet."[15]

Another source of Epstein's visual skepticism is Bergson's philosophy. This might at first appear to be an erroneous claim, given that Bergson was famously critical of the modern scientific argument that reality is very different from the way it appears to human vision. In *Matter and Memory,* Bergson sought a philosophical justification for the common sense belief that "matter exists just as it is perceived. "[16] Nevertheless, even for Bergson human sight does not perceive reality as it really is, although in his view it gets closer to doing so than it does for modern science. Bergson gives a number of reasons this is so. For one, we rarely if ever have a pure, unmediated perception of reality because memory interferes.[17] But even if we were able to give "every form of memory" and obtain "a vision of matter both immediate and instantaneous," this would not mean that we would be able to see the true nature of reality. For while human perception according to Bergson does not add anything to what it perceives, as it does according to the doctrine of secondary qualities, it does subtract something—namely, everything that the object being perceived, what Bergson in *Matter and Memory* calls an image, is connected to throughout time and space.[18] Hence, Bergson tends to talk about perception as an act of isolating what is perceived from its surroundings, by which he means what precedes and follows it temporally, and everything it spatially interacts with throughout the universe:

> I should convert [objective reality] into representation if I could isolate it, especially if I could isolate its shell. . . . It [is] necessary, not to throw more light on the object, but, on the contrary, to obscure some of its aspects, to diminish it by the greater part of itself, so that the remainder, instead of being encased in its surroundings as a *thing,* should detach itself from them as a *picture.* . . . [Objects] become "perceptions" by their very isolation.[19]

In *Creative Evolution,* Bergson describes the objects we perceive as being "cut out of the stuff of nature by our *perception,*" as if perception were a pair of scissors.[20]

Why does human perception isolate or cut out the objects it perceives? It does so because "to perceive all the influences from all the points of all bodies would be to descend to the condition of a material object."[21] In *Matter and Memory,* Bergson proposes an antirepresentationalist theory of perception, arguing that perception consists not of an internal representation of the external world but the stimulation of the brain and nervous system of a living creature by the external world. This stimulation is no different from the interactions taking place between all objects all of the time throughout the universe, and in this sense, all objects "perceive" all other objects, which is why Bergson calls them "images."[22] Humans, however, are different from other objects because they have free will. "Conscious perception signifies choice,"[23] and we choose what to perceive based on practical necessity, suppressing "all those parts of objects in which their functions find no interest."[24]

It is for this reason that Bergson believes that "to perceive is to immobilize" and he uses his famous analogy between perception and photography. Perception cuts out objects from their temporal becoming and the spatial whole of which they are a part, much like a still camera does. It is also for this reason that Bergson claims in *Creative Evolution* that the cinema cannot represent the mobile nature of reality and he characterizes human seeing and knowing as "cinematographic." Just as the cinema creates the impression of movement artificially through a succession of still photographs arranged uniformly on a strip of celluloid, so human "perception, intellection, language . . . take snapshots, as it were, of the passing reality," which we "string" together "on a becoming, abstract, uniform, and invisible." Both the cinema and human perception therefore merely imitate mobile reality through joining a series of immobile representations of reality, "instead of attaching ourselves to the inner becoming of things."[25] For Bergson, this failure, although understandable from a practical point of view, has pernicious consequences, for it means that we are cut off from the "depths of life" of the universe around us, "the vital process" of unpredictable mobility that pulsates, unseen by us, throughout reality, connecting everything to everything else, and we therefore tend, especially in modernity, to fall prey to lifeless, mechanistic forms of knowledge and behavior.[26]

We have already seen evidence of Bergson's influence on Epstein in his claim that human vision cannot see the essential mobility of reality, although, in arguing that the cinema can reveal mobility, Epstein departs, as Gilles Deleuze does, from Bergson's theory. We will encounter Bergson's influence at work again in Epstein's arguments about the cinema and time in chapter 2. Epstein also, like Bergson, believed that even though the naked human eye fails to see the true nature of reality people are not forever unable to access reality. Both drew on the Romantic tradition to argue that artists, in particular, possess a special mental power that enables them to overcome the limitations of the senses. Bergson tended to refer to this power as "intuition," while Epstein, drawing on the language of associationist psychology that was popular in his day, called it the "subconscious." Nevertheless, the powers Epstein attributes to this mental capacity betray his debt to Romanticism.

As Stuart Liebman has shown, in his writings on experimental poetry Epstein argues that the mental faculty of the subconscious is capable of a knowledge of reality superior to that of the conscious intellect. For Epstein, Liebman says, the subconscious can "grasp . . . the essential structure of the objective world."[27] The subconscious, unlike the conscious intellect, is able to transcend the spatial and temporal limitations of sensory perception and external physical appearances and penetrate the internal essence or "being" of objects. It is this power that is often attributed to artists and other seers in Romanticism. For example, William R. Paulson has shown how the figure of the visionary possesses this power in Balzac's novels: "What is here [in *Facino Cane* (1836)] named intuition is described as a doubling or raising to a second power; it is a vision that goes beyond sensation and description, not only seizing the objects accessible to the senses, but also appropriating to a visual order the soul, the symbolic charge, the hidden essence."[28]

In his film theory, Epstein attributes this power to the movie camera, call-ing it "photogénie," the revelation of the inner "personality" of objects.[29] He also often uses terms such as "cinematic telepathy" to describe the relation between the viewer and what is depicted in the cinematic image.[30] Such terms perfectly encapsulate the Romantic ideal of a mental power capable of a di-rect, super-sensory knowledge of reality. "The film," he writes elsewhere, "is nothing but a relay between the source of nervous energy [in the film] and the auditorium which breathes its radiance."[31]

Epstein attempts to put this theory into practice in some of his films, espe-cially in his late silent masterpiece *The Fall of the House of Usher* (1928). This film is usually classified as an example of cinematic Impressionism, the 1920s French avant-garde film movement to which Epstein contributed so much and certainly it is to some extent.[32] Richard Abel, however, has suggested that the film signals a new direction in Epstein's filmmaking, although he is unsure of what, precisely, this direction consists of.[33] It becomes clearer when one views the film within the context of the theoretical influences on Epstein that I have just described, and the skepticism about human vision they licensed. For whereas Impressionist films typically employ techniques of cinematography, editing, and mise-en-scene to represent the subjective mental and perceptual states of their characters, *The Fall of the House of Usher* also uses these tech-niques to escape the limitations of human vision and consciousness and pen-etrate behind the surface appearance of objects to reveal a Bergsonian, mobile reality that the characters in the film are unable to see. Indeed, the film can be interpreted as an allegory of Bergson's claim that "to perceive is to immobi-lize" as well as immobilization's pernicious consequences.

The film tells the story of Roderick Usher, who is attempting to "immo-bilize" his wife, to isolate her both by keeping her secluded in his ancestral mansion (fig. 1.1) and by obsessively trying to capture her likeness in a still portrait he is painting of her. That he is succeeding is explicitly represented in the film through the superimposition of the living Madeline onto the painting, as if she were trapped inside it, cut off from her surroundings (fig. 1.2), and the pronounced tendency toward inertia in the first part of the film, which is created both by the use of slow-motion shots of the characters inside the ancestral home and by the slow movements of the actors. This tendency toward inertia is coun-teracted by an opposite tendency toward mobility in the environment around the characters, as if it were animated by an unseen presence. This is especially true in the ancestral home, with the constantly billowing drapes adorning its walls (fig. 1.3), the piles of books and papers falling over (fig. 1.4), and the seemingly unmotivated camera movements through its corridors, which punctuate the nar-rative. Roderick sometimes forgets his obsession with painting Madeline's por-trait and instead plays his mandolin, shots of which are intercut with shots of the natural environment—trees, fields, water—surrounding the mansion as if to suggest that, at these moments at least, Roderick is able to escape the isolation of his home and obsessive painting and feel a kinship with the living world around him. However, the closer Roderick comes to finishing his painting, to immobi-lizing Madeline, the sicker she becomes, as if her life is being drained from her.

The physician attending Madeline, as a man of science, and Roderick's visiting friend, who is both short-sighted and hard of hearing, are unable to diagnose what is truly wrong with her—the fact that Roderick is immobilizing her in an image, much like sensory perception does according to Bergson.

Figure 1.1. Exterior shot of the Usher mansion in *The Fall of the House of Usher* (Jean Epstein, 1928).

Figure 1.2. Roderick and the doctor discuss Madeline in front of her portrait.

Figure 1.3. The billowing drapes inside the Usher mansion.

Figure 1.4. Books and papers
fall over of their own accord.

When Madeline appears to die, Roderick changes. First, he abandons his
solipsistic obsession with painting her portrait and resists a new form of her
immobilization, the attempt on the part of the physician and friend to nail her
coffin shut (fig. 1.5). Second, he becomes highly sensitive to the mobile environment around him as he awaits any sign that Madeline might still be alive,
so that, as one of the inter-titles puts it, "His nerves at breaking point . . . the
slightest sound exasperated him." Epstein conveys the strange, inhuman quality of this animistic environment by cutting to close-ups of two mating toads
(fig. 1.6) and an owl as Madeline's coffin is being nailed shut. There follows
a remarkable sequence in which shots of Roderick's tense, expectant face and
body (fig. 1.7) are intercut with shots of a nearby grandfather clock (fig. 1.8).
Epstein's camera penetrates behind the exterior of the clock, revealing, in extreme close-ups, the movements of the clock's internal mechanism (fig. 1.9),
its gears, pendulum, and bell, which, as it chimes, releases particles of dust
(fig. 1.10). Roderick cannot *see* the mobility of the internal mechanism of the
clock and the dust particles, but he can *sense* it, as is conveyed by the cuts to
his reactions. Finally, immobility and death are overcome by mobility and life,
as an electrical storm begins, the curtains billow more and more violently, and
the camera moves increasingly rapidly along the hallways strewn with leaves.
As the ancestral home begins to burn down, Madeline's portrait along with it
(fig. 1.11), Madeline rises from her tomb (fig. 1.12), no longer immobilized by
coffin, mansion, or portrait, and she, Roderick, and his friend escape back into
living nature.

Thus, the new direction Epstein takes in this film is to explore stylistic
techniques often used to represent human subjectivity in Impressionist film
proper (camera movement, extreme close-ups, superimposition) to depict, as
well, a Bergsonian, mobile reality surrounding the characters. Motivating this
new direction, which Epstein pursued further in some of his non-Impressionist,
quasi-documentary sound films, is his belief that the human eye cannot see
the true nature of reality, its mobility. For the characters in the film can at best
intuit, rather than perceive, this mobile reality, and we viewers are only able to
see it because the cinema can escape the limitations of human perception and
reveal it to us.

Figure 1.5. Roderick attempts
to prevent Madeline's coffin
(visible at the bottom of the shot)
from being nailed shut.

Figure 1.6. Mating toads.

Figure 1.7. Roderick waits,
sensing the mobility around him.

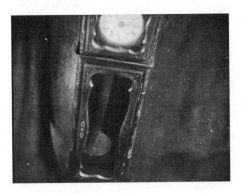

Figure 1.8. The grandfather
clock.

29

Figure 1.9. The internal mechanism of the clock.

Figure 1.10. Extreme close up of dust falling off the bell inside the clock.

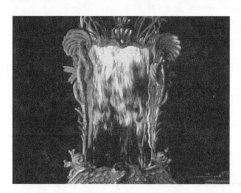

Figure 1.11. Madeline's portrait burning.

Figure 1.12. Madeline resurrected.

II

Of the four film theorists whose work I am examining in the first two chapters of this book, visual skepticism probably exerted the most influence over Dziga Vertov. This is abundantly evident in his writings of the 1920s and 1930s, and it informs many of his major arguments as well as his filmmaking. Indeed, in Vertov's work, visual skepticism often takes the from of an outright contempt for the naked human eye.

Take, for example, Vertov's hostility to fiction film, which is a well-known feature of his theory and practice. Like other Soviets of his generation, Vertov believed that the cinema could potentially play a major role in the construction of a new, socialist society after the Bolshevik revolution of 1917. And, again like others, for him this role consisted of depicting social reality as theorized by Marxist-Leninism, as well as of generating enthusiasm for the new society being built upon this theory. But unlike most others, Vertov argued that fiction films, even the avant-garde fiction films of someone like Sergei Eisenstein, could not play this role. Cinema had to be nonfiction, or "nonplayed."

Vertov gives a number of reasons for his hostility to fiction film. For one thing, fiction or "played" films typically employ a written scenario or script in their production. They therefore violate two major tenets of Vertov's theory and practice. Like other classical film theorists, Vertov argues that the cinema as a medium should be independent of other media, in particular theater and literature. Only those formal and stylistic techniques unique to the cinema should be used by the filmmaker: "WE are cleansing *kinochestvo* of foreign matter—of music, literature, and theater; we seek our own rhythm, one lifted from nowhere else, and we find it in the movements of things."[34] The use of a written scenario in the production of fiction films constitutes for Vertov an intolerable intrusion by literature, a "foreign" medium, into the cinema. He therefore scathingly dismisses fiction films as "mere literary skeleton[s] covered with a film-skin."[35]

The written scenario also violates the Constructivist tenet of a "culture of materials" to which Vertov adhered, a tenet which insists upon the role of the raw material of an art work in shaping its final form. This Constructivist tenet is summarized by El Lissitzky in a retrospective essay on Russian architecture written in 1929: "The second way of looking at the world, in terms of material, required not merely observation but also the tactile apprehension of things. The specific qualities of the respective materials served as a starting point for the development of the form."[36] Vertov, defining the raw material of the cinema as "the phenomena of life," argues that the filmmaker must proceed "from the material to the film-object."[37] The collection of the raw material for film objects during the act of filming, and the organization of this material in the editing room, cannot be predetermined. Instead, the form of a film has to grow out of the specific qualities of the raw material. This sequence of production, and the Constructivist tenet underpinning it, are by definition violated if the film object is predetermined by a written scenario before shooting, as it is in fiction filmmaking. Vertov also routinely appeals to the argument, later employed by

Bertolt Brecht, that works of fiction diminish or destroy an audience's capacity to think rationally because of the emotions they arouse: "Kino-drama clouds the eye and the brain with a sweet fog."[38]

Just as important, but much less noted, an additional reason for Vertov's hostility to fiction film is his distrust of human sight. According to Vertov, a fundamental problem with fiction films, as with all film practices except his own, is that they "copy the work of our eye."[39]

> The death sentence passed in 1919 by the kinoks on all films, with no exceptions, holds for the present as well. The most scrupulous examination does not reveal a single film, a single artistic experiment, properly directed to the emancipation of the camera, which is reduced to a state of pitiable slavery, of subordination to the imperfections and the shortsightedness of the human eye.[40]

In other words, so great is Vertov's distrust of human vision, and so intense his desire to depart from it, that it leads him to reject all film practices that he views as employing "the human eye as crib sheet."[41]

Like Epstein, Vertov believes that human sight is incapable of seeing reality as it really is. Unlike Epstein, it is the true nature of *social* reality, and not so much the *physical* universe, that the eye fails to see. Human eyes are too weak: "The weakness of the human eye is manifest."[42] Only an instrument much more powerful than the eye can reveal social reality, and Vertov views the cinema as being this instrument. The cinema is "more perfect than the human eye"; it "perceives more and better."[43] It enables "the communist decoding of the world," the revelation of "the truth" about social reality "on the screen."[44] Hence, it is only with the invention of the cinema and its liberation from "the crib sheet of the human eye" that people can, for the first time, actually see social reality as it really is: "The eyes of children and adults, the educated as well as the uneducated, are opening, as it were, for the first time. Millions of workers . . . recovered their sight."[45]

According to Vertov, human vision suffers from two fundamental limitations that prevent it from seeing the true nature of social reality, both of which the cinema overcomes. The first prevents people from fully seeing and understanding visual phenomena in general, not just social reality. For according to Vertov, our "perceptions" are disorganized and confusing. He gives as an example stage performances. "The spectator at a ballet follows, in confusion, now the combined group of dancers, now random individual figures, now someone's legs—a series of scattered perceptions, different for each spectator."[46] The cinema is able to overcome this limitation, "bring[ing] clarity into the worker's awareness of the phenomena concerning him and surrounding him,"[47] because of the precision with which editing can be used to organize visual phenomena recorded on film into harmonious patterns—based upon geometrical principles—that can be understood by the viewer.

> Within the *chaos* of movements, running past, away, running into and colliding— the eye, all by itself, enters life.

A day of visual impressions has passed. How is one to construct the impressions of the day into an effective whole, a visual study? If one films everything the eye has seen, the result, of course, will be a *jumble*. If one skillfully edits what's been photographed, the result will be clearer. If one scraps bothersome waste, it will be better still. One obtains an organized memo of the ordinary eye's impressions.[48]

Vertov calls the precise link, achieved on the editing table, between one visual phenomenon and the next "an interval," and he compares the harmonious pattern of intervals created by the editor to a musical phrase conceived of in classical terms.

Intervals (the transitions from one movement to another) are the material, the elements of the art of movement, and by no means the movements themselves. It is they (the intervals) which draw the movement to a kinetic resolution.

The organization of movement is the organization of its elements, or its intervals, into phrases.

In each phrase there is a rise, a high point, and a falling off (expressed in varying degrees) of movement.[49]

Via the precision of editing, the editor can organize what is for the human eye a confusing array of perceptions into ordered, harmonious, and therefore intelligible patterns, overcoming the eye's limitation. To return to the ballet example:

The eye submits to the will of the camera and is directed by it to those successive points of the action that, most succinctly and vividly, bring the film phrase to the height or depth of resolution. . . .

A system of successive movements requires the filming of dancers . . . in the order of their actions, one after another . . . by forceful transfer of the viewer's eye to the successive details that must be seen.

The camera "carries" the film viewer's eyes from arms to legs, from legs to eyes and so on, in the most advantageous sequence, and organizes the details into an orderly montage study.[50]

The second limitation that the human eye suffers from, according to Vertov, is that it is temporally and spatially immobile. It is confined to the present, and it moves through space slowly. The problem with this immobility is that the sort of phenomena that constitute social reality require much greater temporal and spatial mobility in order to be seen, as we shall see in chapter 2. In contrast, the cinema is "free of the limits of time and space," and Vertov repeatedly emphasizes its greater mobility in comparison to the eye: "The position of our bodies while observing or our perception of a certain number of features of a visual phenomenon in a given instant are by no means obligatory limitations for the camera."[51] In terms of space, the cinema can "put together any given points in the universe, no matter where [it has] recorded them."[52] And just as it can traverse large expanses of space quickly (though camera movement) or instantaneously (through editing), so the cinema can move backward and forward in time. This can be achieved by way of editing: "The coffins of national heroes are lowered into the grave (shot in Astrakhan in 1918); the grave is filled in (Kronstadt, 1921); cannon salute (Petrograd, 1920); memorial service, hats are removed (Moscow, 1922)."[53] Or it can be achieved by fast, slow, and reverse motion: "[The camera] experiments, distending time, dissecting movement, or, in contrary fashion, absorbing time within itself, swallowing years, thus schematizing processes of long duration inaccessible to the normal eye."[54] Because of its capacity to move rapidly though space and time, the cinema, Vertov asserts, allows for "the possibility of seeing without limits and distances."[55]

We have seen that Epstein's distrust of human sight was the product of a number of influences: modern science, Bergson's philosophy, and Romanticism. One source of Vertov's visual skepticism is what the historian Richard Stites calls the "cult of the machine," which was particularly influential in the Soviet Union in the 1920s, and idealized the machine as a model of perfection for both society and human beings.[56] Soviet visionaries and reformers of the 1920s, such as Platon Kerzhentsev and Alexei Gastev, envisaged the transformation of human beings into "new people," more perfect because they were more machinelike. While working, these new people would overcome the imperfections of the natural rhythms and gestures of the human body by coordinating and controlling their movements with the precision and efficiency of a machine, ensuring maximum productivity and eliminating wastage of time and energy. Gastev's popular poetry from the 1910s is particularly well known for the way in which it imagines the future as a mechanical utopia in which humans with "nerves of steel" and "muscles like iron rails" work with the precision and efficiency of machines.

While Vertov's relation to the Soviet cult of the machine is, I have argued elsewhere, complex, the ideal of the machine as more perfect than the human body is clearly present in his film theory and practice.[57] In his 1922 manifesto "We," for example, he argues:

> The machine makes us ashamed of man's inability to control himself, but what are we to do if electricity's unerring ways are more exciting to us than the disorderly haste of active men and the corrupting inertia of passive ones?
>
> Saws dancing at a sawmill convey to us a joy more intimate and intelligible than that on human dance floors.
>
> *For his inability to control his movements, WE temporarily exclude man as a subject for film.*
>
> *Our path leads through the poetry of machines, from the bungling citizen to the perfect electric man. . . .*
>
> *The new man,* free of unwieldness and clumsiness, will have the light, precise movements of machines, and he will be the gratifying subject of our films.[58]

The prediction Vertov makes in the final sentence of this quotation comes true in the films he goes on to make after writing this manifesto. In *Man with a Movie Camera* (1929), for example, there is a frenetic sequence that interconnects shots of various types of labor. Close-up shots of film celluloid being spliced and edited are interspersed with close-up shots of typing, writing, a sewing machine, and a newspaper conveyer belt. Typically, only the workers' hands are present in these shots, moving swiftly and with precision, with occasional cuts to their faces as they stare intently down at their work. Within this fast-paced, exuberant sequence, there is a short series of shots of a woman folding cigarette boxes on a wooden block. This series begins with a close-up of a machine sorting and processing similar boxes (fig. 1.13). There is then a cut to a close-up of the woman's hands rapidly folding a box on the wooden stand (fig. 1.14), followed by a cut to her face as she stares downward at her work (fig. 1.15) and throws the completed box over her shoulder onto a pile. The film cuts back and forth between identical shots of the woman's hands and face about five or six times. It then returns to a shot of the box-sorting machine, followed by a final shot of the woman. The woman's movements are identical in each shot, much like the repetitious movements of a machine. And the cuts between her hands and face follow a regular rhythm, like a machine. Each shot of her hands pauses for roughly two seconds as she folds the box, and then the shot of her face as she discards it over her shoulder lasts a single, third second. This pattern is repeated five or six times and its pace accelerated. This worker is endowed with the mechanical rhythm of the box-sorting machine with which she works by the repeated pattern of the editing and by cuts back and forth between the woman and the machine. She is a perfect example of the "new people" envisaged by Gastev, someone who has overcome the imperfections of the human body by imitating the rhythm and movement of the machines around her.

It is this idealization of the machine as more perfect than the human body that constitutes one source of Vertov's hostility to human vision. For just as Vertov decries the "disorderly" movements of the human body in comparison to the "precise" movements of machines, so, as we have seen, he unfavorably compares the confusion of sight to the organized, harmonious, and therefore intelligible patterns of visual phenomena enabled by the machines of the

Figure 1.13. Sorting machine in *Man with a Movie Camera* (Dziga Vertov, 1929).

Figure 1.14. Worker's hands.

Figure 1.15. Worker's face.

cinema—the editing table and the movie camera. In other words, Vertov extends into the realm of perception the terms used by the Soviet cult of the machine to describe the superiority of the machine over the human body in the context of movement and labor—"precision," "control," the elimination of waste, and so on.

Vertov's idealization of the machine and his faith in modernization, technological progress, and science to some extent sets him apart from Epstein and his Romantic belief in the subconscious as superior to the conscious intellect, as well as from Balázs and Kracauer who, as we will discover, also owe a major debt to Romanticism. Yet, even though Vertov's rationalism makes him the most anti-Romantic of the film theorists in the revelationist tradition proper, he still shares with them the view that human sight is unreliable and the cinema is capable of revealing the true nature of reality by escaping the eye's limitations. His theory and practice might also share with Epstein's a theoretical source for his conception of these limitations, namely, Bergsonianism, which, as Hillary Fink has shown, exerted a major influence over Soviet artists in the 1920s.[59] This is perhaps why Gilles Deleuze argues that Vertov "realizes the materialist programme of the first chapter of [Bergson's] *Matter and Memory* through the cinema."[60] By this, Deleuze seems to mean that Vertov's films depict social reality very much like physical reality as described by Bergson's metaphysics, a ceaselessly changing reality in which everything is constantly acting on everything else and is in turn acted on by everything else throughout time and space. As Deleuze puts it: "Whether there were machines, landscapes, buildings or men [being filmed] was of little consequence: each—even the most charming peasant woman or the most touching child—was presented as a material system in perpetual interaction."[61] In Vertov's cinema, argues Deleuze, "everything is at the service of variation and interaction."[62] His films are able to represent this ceaseless interaction because of the cinema's mobility, its capacity, through camera movement and editing, to move from "a point where an action begins to the limit of the reaction, as it fills the interval between the two, crossing the universe and beating in time to its intervals."[63] For Deleuze, following Bergson's theory of the limitations of human perception and echoing a central theme of this book, this capacity to reveal actions and reactions throughout space and time means that the cinema in Vertov's hands escapes its limitations and is therefore superhuman. "This is not a human eye—even an improved one. For, although the human eye can surmount some of its limitations with the help of contraptions and instruments, there is one which it cannot surmount, since it is its own condition of possibility."[64] This condition is, of course, immobility, because as we have seen, for Bergson "to perceive is to immobilize." Vertov's cinema, in Deleuze's view, reveals within the domain of social reality the surroundings that are of necessity subtracted when human perception cuts what it perceives out of reality: everything it interacts with throughout the universe spatially and temporally.

Whether or not one agrees with Deleuze's Bergsonian interpretation of Vertov's films (as John MacKay has astutely pointed out, this interpretation ignores the human contribution to editing that is explicitly represented in *Man with a Movie Camera* through the shots of Vertov's wife, Elizaveta Svilova, at the editing table editing the very film we are watching[65]), in his writings Vertov clearly conceives of the naked eye as immobile in the sense that it is confined to the present and that it moves through space slowly. Human vision thereby fails to perceive the connections between things, an argument that strongly echoes Bergson's theory of the limitations of sight. Due to the precision of editing and its mobility, according to Vertov, the cinema is able to escape these perceptual limitations and reveal the true nature of social reality.

III

In *Theory of the Film* (1948), his third and last book of film theory, Béla Balázs argued that "The already once accomplished and then again lost achievements of the silent film are about to be revalued and restored."[66] As this claim implies, Balázs was very much a silent-film theorist. His film theory was largely predicated on cinema lacking synchronized sound, especially dialogue. When synchronized sound did arrive in the late 1920s, Balázs felt that much of what was of value about the cinema as an art had been lost, and he had not changed his mind by the time he wrote *Theory of the Film* twenty years later.

Balázs's continuing attachment to silent film was due, at least in part, to the sort of distrust of human vision that we saw at work in the theories of Epstein and Vertov. However, Balázs's visual skepticism (and, as we will see later, Kracauer's) differs in at least one important respect from Epstein's and Vertov's. Like them, Balázs argues that the cinema reveals truths about reality invisible to the naked eye: "In the silent film facial expression, isolated from its surroundings [by the close-up], seemed to penetrate to a strange new dimension of the soul. It revealed to us a new world—the world of microphysiognomy which could not otherwise be seen with the naked eye or in everyday life" (TTF 65). And, again like Epstein and Vertov, Balázs compares the cinema to other visual technologies, in particular the microscope.

> The technique of the close-up . . . was able to make us feel nerve-rackingly the sultry tension underneath the superficial calm; the fierce storms raging under the surface were made tangible by mere microscopic movements, by the displacement of a hair. . . . The micro-tragedies in the peace and quiet of ordinary families were shown as deadly battles, just as the microscope shows the fierce struggles of micro-organisms in a drop of water. (TTF 84–85)

But unlike Epstein and Vertov, Balázs argues that it is, in part, a historical limitation that sight suffers from, a limitation from which it can potentially recover. For Epstein and Vertov, the eye's inability to see the true nature of reality is due to innate handicaps that cannot be overcome (except perhaps by evolution), such as its immobility (Epstein), and its disorganized and therefore confusing perceptions (Vertov). But for Balázs, people have forgotten how to see due to historically specific forces at work in modernity.

According to Balázs, because of the invention of the printing press, the printed word has become the dominant medium through which people express their inner, mental lives in modernity, giving rise to what he calls a "word culture": "The printing press has grown to be the main bridge over which the more remote interhuman spiritual exchanges take place and the soul has been concentrated and crystallized chiefly in the word" (TTF 41). One consequence is that people have almost totally lost the capacity to use their faces and bodies to express the inner: "The animals that do not chew lose their teeth. In the epoch of word culture we made little use of the expressive powers of our body and have therefore partly lost that power" (TTF 42). The loss of this capacity means that the dimension of "nonrational emotions" that used to be expressed by the face and body can no longer be expressed, for language can only communicate rational concepts: "We had, however, when we neglected the body as a means of expression, lost more than mere corporal power of expression. That which was to have been expressed was also narrowed down by this neglect. For it is not the same spirit, not the same soul that is expressed once in words and once in gestures" (TTF 42). The result is a spiritual impoverishment in modernity. The nonrational emotional realm that can only be expressed by the face and body remains unexpressed, leaving just the "rational, conceptual culture" of the word (TTF 43).

This in turn has an impact on vision, and it is in describing this impact that Balázs's claims about the limitations of human sight emerge. People have forgotten how to see the face and body as expressive of the inner in the word culture of modernity, according to Balázs, because they are no longer used to express the inner. Meanwhile, it is because the cinema lacks synchronized sound in the silent era, and actors are therefore forced to relearn how to express the inner through facial expression and bodily behavior, that Balázs in his early film theory believes that the cinema is bringing about the evolution of new perceptual abilities in humans. People are once again learning how to read the language of the face and body by watching actors in silent films.

> Now we are beginning to remember and re-learn this tongue. It is still clumsy and primitive and very far removed as yet from the refinements of word art. But already it is beginning to be able sometimes to express things which escape the artists of the word. How much of human thought would remain unexpressed if we had no music! The now developing art of facial expression and gesture will bring just as many submerged contents to the surface. Although these human experiences are not rational, conceptual contents, they are nevertheless neither vague nor blurred, but as clear and unequivocal as is music. Thus the inner man, too, will become visible. (TTF 42)

Human vision therefore suffers from a historical limitation, according to Balázs, one that is specific to the word culture of modernity. Because it is only historical, as opposed to innate, the eye can potentially recover from it, and this is precisely what Balázs believed was starting to happen in the silent era. The cinema, he thought, was reeducating people about how to use and understand the language of facial expression and bodily behavior. The nonrational emotional realm of the inner was becoming visible again for the first time since the invention of the printing press. With the arrival of synchronized sound, however, all of this changed. Actors reverted to spoken language to express the inner, thereby reinforcing the word culture of modernity, and the new education being offered by cinema in the silent era was cut short—hence, Balázs's lifelong attachment to silent film.

Balázs's claims about the limitations of human vision constitute an idiosyncratic version of what can be called the modern subjectivity theory, which has its roots in Romanticism. This theory argues that various forces in modernity—principally science, technology, and the penetration of "instrumental reason" into all spheres of human existence—have had a profound effect on humans. These forces have altered the way that the average person's mind works, giving rise to a distinctively modern form of consciousness that is overly rationalistic and divorced from the senses, the body, and nature in general.

Rudolf Arnheim summarizes key elements of this theory at the beginning of
Art and Visual Perception:

> We are neglecting the gift of comprehending things by what our senses tell us
> about them. Concept is split from percept, and thought moves among abstractions.
> Our eyes are being reduced to instruments by which to measure and identify—hence a
> dearth of ideas that can be expressed in images and an incapacity to discover meaning
> in what we see. Naturally we feel lost in the presence of objects that make sense only
> to undiluted vision, and we look for help to the more familiar medium of words.[67]

We can distinguish between several claims in this familiar generalization about modern subjectivity. First is the argument that modern subjectivity is divided into two realms, the mental and the physical ("concept is split
from percept"). Second is the suggestion that the mental realm dominates the
physical senses, including the eyes, and is overly rationalistic ("our eyes are
being reduced to instruments by which to measure and identify"). As a result,
humans, on average, no longer attend to what the senses have to teach them
independently of the mental realm ("we are neglecting the gift of comprehend-
ing things by what our senses tell us about them"). Finally, there is the claim
that people now typically "look for help" in the more familiar mental realm of
language, rather than the physical realm of the senses, because we no longer
know how to learn from "undiluted vision"—in other words, vision functioning independently of the overly rational mind.

Clearly, this theory evinces a deep skepticism about vision, arguing that
humans cannot see reality directly because they subsume what they see under
abstract concepts provided by language. Balázs modifies this theory by placing
an intermediary stage—the use of language in place of the face and body to
express the inner—in between the tendency to "look for help in the more familiar medium of words" and the failure to attend to what the senses have to
teach independently of language. It is the use of language in place of the face
and body, due to the dominance of language in the word culture of modernity,
that results in humans forgetting how to see the face and body of another as
expressive of mind, according to Balázs.

As we shall see in a moment, this did not mean that for Balázs the nonrational emotional realm expressed by the face and body once again became
submerged and unexpressed when synchronized sound arrived, as it had been
before the invention of cinema. For vision also suffers from another limitation.
Humans, Balázs argues again and again, are very bad at noticing details. They
look at reality "as a concert-goer ignorant of music listens to an orchestra playing a symphony. All he hears is the leading melody, all the rest is blurred into
a general murmur. Only those can really understand and enjoy the music who
can hear the contrapuntal architecture of each part in the score. This is how we
see life: only its leading melody meets the eye" (TTF 55).

It is not clear from the above passage, or Balázs's film theory in general,
whether Balázs believes the inability to notice details is an innate physiological

limitation of normal human vision or just a bad visual habit that can be corrected. But either way, he thinks it is a limitation of the naked eye, and one that, he argues, the cinema overcomes, primarily through the close-up: "But a good film with its close-ups reveals the most hidden parts in our polyphonous life, and teaches us to see the intricate visual details of life as one reads an orchestral score" (TTF 55). Because it isolates and magnifies whatever it films, the close-up reveals details that are invisible to sight: "An ant-heap is lifeless if seen from a distance, but at close quarters it is teeming with busy life. The grey, dull texture of everyday life shows in its microdramatics many profoundly moving happenings, if we look at it carefully enough in close-up" (TTF 86).

Due to the fact that the naked eye cannot see details, it is unable to see the inner expressed in the details of the faces and bodies of others. In contrast, because the close-up isolates and magnifies these details, the inner manifested in the details of a face or body filmed in close-up is revealed to the viewer: "But in the isolated close-up of the film we can see to the bottom of a soul by means of such tiny movements of facial muscles which even the most observant partner would never perceive" (TTF 63). Thus, the realm of the inner expressed by the face and body did not once again become submerged and unexpressed when synchronized sound arrived. Although this happened to some extent, the use of the close-up in sound film ensured that this realm of the inner remained partially visible, even though actors were no longer forced to use their faces and bodies to express themselves because of synchronized dialogue. The close-up, by isolating and magnifying the details of the faces and bodies it films, can reveal the inner expressed unintentionally in those details—details that the naked eye cannot see unaided.

IV

Kracauer's claims about the limitations of human vision also constitute a version of the modern subjectivity theory, although a more straightforward one than Balázs's. Like our other film theorists, Kracauer claims that the cinema reveals truths about reality invisible to sight, such as "objects too small to be readily noticed or even perceived by the naked eye."[68] And, again like other revelationists, he makes the familiar comparison between the cinema and visual technologies such as the microscope: "In its preoccupation with the small the cinema is comparable to science. Like science, it breaks down material phenomena into tiny particles, thereby sensitizing us to the tremendous energies accumulated in the microscopic configurations of matter" (TF 50). But like Balázs, and unlike Epstein and Vertov, for Kracauer it is a historical limitation specific to modernity that vision suffers from, and, unlike Balázs, Kracauer does not argue that people have forgotten how to see.

According to Kracauer, one of the fundamental features of modernity is "abstractness" (TF 291), and he explains what he means by this term by referring to the sciences: "Most sciences do not deal with the objects of ordinary experience but abstract from them certain elements which they then process in various ways. Thus the objects are stripped of the qualities which give them 'all their poignancy and preciousness' (Dewey)" (TF 292).

This lack of concern with qualities is what constitutes the abstractness of the sciences, and Kracauer argues that, due to the enormous influence of the sciences in modernity, "our way of thinking and our whole attitude toward reality are conditioned by the principles from which science proceeds," including the principle of abstractness: "the abstractness inherent in [the sciences] cannot but influence our habits of thought" (TF 292). Thus, for Kracauer, the average human in modernity, like a scientist, does not attend to the qualities of objects: "scientific and technological abstractions condition the minds most effectively; and they all refer us to physical phenomena, while at the same time luring us away from their qualities" (TF 298).

Kracauer points to what he believes to be several pernicious consequences of abstractness. One is that it "impedes practically all direct efforts to revamp religion and establish a consensus of beliefs" (TF 294). As any reader of Kracauer will know, one of the features of modernity that preoccupied him throughout his life and that he repeatedly bemoaned in his writings is the lack of ideological unity in modern life, the absence of the sort of "binding norms" (TF 287) that were supposedly provided by religion in premodern times. As he puts it in his first published article in 1915 when describing the state of Germany over the previous ten years, "Above all else, the most important need of the soul, the religious, lay broken; there were no living, universally binding beliefs that expressed our essence."[69] And forty-five years later, in *Theory of Film,* Kracauer wrote under the subtitle "Ruins of ancient beliefs" (taken from Durkheim):

> From the nineteenth century on practically all thinkers of consequence, no matter how much they differed in approach and outlook, have agreed that beliefs once widely held—beliefs that were embraced by the whole of the person and covered life in its wholeness—have been inexorably waning. They not only acknowledge this fact but speak of it with an assurance which is palpably founded on inner experience. It is as if they felt in their very bones the breakdown of binding norms. (TF 287)

"Man in our society is ideologically shelterless" (TF 288), Kracauer laments, and he often uses metaphors of fragmentation to describe the supposed loss of shared beliefs in modernity, in contradistinction to the supposed wholeness provided by shared beliefs such as religion in premodern times.

According to Kracauer, it is, in part, the abstractness of modernity that prevents the restoration of the ideological wholeness characteristic of premodern life. When humans "try to get in touch with mental entities," such as ideological beliefs, "we reduce them to abstractions as colorless as the noise to which radio music is commonly being reduced" (TF 293). We do this by "passing [mental entities] off as derivatives of psychological dispositions," and Kracauer cites Freudian psychoanalysis and "depth psychology" in general as examples (TF 293). We also do this through "relativistic reduction," the "realiz[ation] that everything can be viewed from more than one angle" (TF 293).

Because we compare the various ideologies that are on offer in modernity, we "run the risk of missing the very essences of the diverse value systems to which we are exposed. Our interest in their comparable elements interferes with our readiness to absorb any such system for its own sake" (TF 294).

But it is not just our relation to mental phenomena, such as ideological beliefs, that is affected by the abstractness of modernity, according to Kracauer. It is also our relation to physical phenomena, and it is in characterizing this relation that Kracauer's claims about the limitations of human vision emerge. Because we do not attend to the qualities of objects, he argues, we do not see them. "Physical reality," including the phenomena people typically encounter in everyday life in modern societies—"streets, faces, railway stations" (TF 299)—has "remained largely invisible" in modernity, he claims, and this is due to abstractness. "The truly decisive reason for the elusiveness of physical reality is the habit of abstract thinking we have acquired under the reign of science and technology," which leads us to "eliminate the qualities of things" (TF 299–300). Hence, we live with only "a shadowy awareness of things in their fullness" (TF 291). We touch "reality only with the fingertips" (TF 294).

Thus, as it does for Balázs, human vision suffers from a historical limitation for Kracauer, one that is specific to modernity. Unlike Balázs, though, Kracauer does not argue that the eye used to be free in premodern times of the limitation it suffers in modernity. It is not that humans have forgotten how to see the qualities of objects for Kracauer, as they have forgotten how to see the face and body as expressive of mind for Balázs. According to Kracauer, in premodern times, sight suffered from the same limitation as it does in modernity, but for a different reason. Whereas in modernity it is abstractness that prevents people from seeing the qualities of things, in premodern times it was ideologies, such as religion. "It should be remembered that physical nature has been persistently veiled by ideologies relating its manifestations to some total aspect of the universe" (TF 299). For Kracauer, therefore, "physical reality" has always been "largely invisible" to humans, first due to ideology in premodern times and now due to abstractness in modernity.

As in Balázs's film theory, because abstractness is only a historical, as opposed to an innate, limitation, the human eye can potentially recover from it, and it is precisely such a recovery that Kracauer believes the cinema effects. Because the camera's mechanical nature allows it to record and reproduce what is in front of it—including all of the qualities of objects that are supposedly invisible to people in modernity due to abstractness—regardless of what the filmmaker thinks or believes is in front of it, it reveals a physical reality that has never before been seen by humans due to abstraction in modernity and ideology in premodern times. "Film renders visible what we did not, or perhaps even could not, see before its advent. It effectively assists us in discovering the material world with its psychophysical correspondences. We literally redeem this world from its dormant state, its state of virtual nonexistence, by endeavouring to experience it through the camera" (TF 300). Hence, Kracauer's *Theory of Film* is subtitled *The Redemption of Physical Reality*: cinema redeems physical reality from its invisible state.

Cinema only does this, though, if used in a certain way, and *Theory of Film* is to some extent a manifesto advocating a specific way of using the cinema. Kracauer follows many traditional film historians in arguing that there have been two major traditions of filmmaking in the history of cinema. The first, which he calls the realistic tendency and which is exemplified by the films of the Lumière Brothers, uses the cinema's recording properties to reproduce reality. The second, which he refers to as the formative tendency and which is exemplified by Méliès's films, uses properties of cinema such as editing to transform reality according to the filmmaker's vision. Kracauer acknowledges that the second tradition conforms to the standard definition of art in the twentieth century as necessarily involving the transformation of reality by the artist. It was, of course, this definition of art that informed the first wave of film theory and history from the 1910s through the 1930s, which was in large measure aimed at rebutting the claim that cinema, like photography, is not an art because it can only record and reproduce reality.[70] Kracauer, however, departs from this first wave of film theory and history by arguing that when this standard definition of art is applied to the cinema, it "thwarts the cinema's intrinsic possibilities. If for reasons of aesthetic purity films influenced by the traditional arts prefer to disregard actual physical reality, they miss an opportunity reserved for the cinematic medium" (TF 301). As this statement suggests, Kracauer was a medium-specific theorist, meaning that he believed that "each medium has a specific nature which invites certain kinds of communications while obstructing others" (TF 3). According to him, the recording and reproducing of reality is one of the cinema's essential properties, part of its "specific nature." Thus, only films that record and reproduce reality "may claim aesthetic validity" (TF 37). This, in turn, means that the traditional definition of art as necessarily involving the transformation of reality by the artist does not apply to the cinema (and photography). If cinema is an art, it is an "art with a difference. Indeed, along with photography, film is the only art which exhibits its raw material" (TF 302).[71]

Kracauer, however, does not completely reject the standard definition of art and the formative tendency in filmmaking that is believed to exemplify it. Instead, like André Bazin before him and Victor Perkins after him, Kracauer tries to find a rapprochement between this definition and the requirement that films record and reproduce reality by arguing that "the formative tendency . . . does not have to conflict with the realistic tendency. Quite the contrary, it may help substantiate and fulfill it" (TF 16). Just as Bazin had argued that filmmakers such as Jean Renoir had creatively found ways to better record and reproduce reality, discovering and developing techniques such as the long take and the shot in depth, so Kracauer argues that the formal and stylistic properties of the photographic and cinematic mediums, as well as the photographer and filmmaker's creativity, can be employed in the service of better recording and reproducing reality: "Provided his choices are governed by his determination to record and reveal nature, he is entirely justified in selecting motif, frame, lens, filter, emulsion and grain according to his sensibilities" (TF 15). Hence, the filmmaker's formative tendency plays a role in the type of filmmaking Kracauer is advocating.

But this formative tendency must be subordinated to recording and reproducing reality: "What counts is the 'right' mixture of his realist loyalties and formative endeavours—a mixture, that is, in which the latter, however strongly developed, surrender their independence to the former" (TF 16).

Thus, in *Theory of Film,* Kracauer advocates a certain way of using the cinema, one in which the formative is subordinated to the realistic. He does so, in part, because he is a medium-specific theorist. He believes that recording and reproducing is one of the cinema's essential properties. However, he also does so because of his distrust of human vision, his claim that, due to the abstractness of modernity, humans do not see the qualities of objects and therefore have only a "shadowy awareness" of physical reality. If cinema is to redeem physical reality for people, if it is to render "visible what we did not, or perhaps even could not, see before its advent," it must reproduce reality rather than transform it according to the filmmaker's vision: "in order to make us experience physical reality, films must show what they picture" (TF 300).

Using the cinema to record and reproduce reality not only changes our relation to physical reality by revealing the qualities of objects, according to Kracauer. It also changes our relation to mental phenomena, including ideology. As we have seen, for Kracauer the abstractness of modernity prevents the restoration of the ideological wholeness characteristic of premodern times. Thus, he concludes that a step toward this restoration would be taken if the abstractness of modernity were to be eliminated: "if we want to assimilate values that delimit our horizon we must first rid ourselves of that abstractness as best we can" (TF 296). One way of eliminating abstractness is by revealing the qualities of objects to sight: "We can limit our all but compulsive indulgence in abstractions only if we restore to objects the qualities which, as Dewey says, give them 'their poignancy and preciousness.' The remedy for the kind of abstractness which befalls minds under the impact of science is experience—the experience of things in their concreteness" (TF 296). In as much as cinema enables us to "experience things in their concreteness," it weakens if not destroys the power of abstractness over our minds and bodies, thereby not only "assist[ing] us in discovering the material world," but helping us to take a step toward regaining ideological wholeness, toward escaping the "spiritual nakedness" of modernity.

As should be evident, Kracauer's arguments about the limitations of human vision are a straightforward version of the modern subjectivity theory. His basic claims—about the abstract nature of the modern mind, about the failure of humans in modernity to attend to "what our senses tell us about" the world independently of abstract categories—are familiar themes from this theory. And it is perhaps because of the influence of this theory, or rather a powerful version of it that he encounters in the United States, that Kracauer's conception of the cinema as a revelatory technology changes during his lifetime. In his early film theory of the 1920s and early 1930s, Kracauer argued that it is truths about social reality, rather than physical reality, that are revealed by the cinema to the viewer. And it is not so much what the cinema represents, but rather how it represents it, that is revelatory. As we have seen, throughout his life, Kracauer lamented the supposed loss of ideological wholeness in modernity. In his early film theory, he claimed that the cinema reveals to us our modern condition of ideological fragmentation through the fragmentary, distracting, superficial nature of the sensory experience it offers to viewers. As he puts it: "Here, in pure externality, the audience encounters itself; its own reality is revealed in the fragmented sequence of splendid sense impressions. Were this reality to remain hidden from the viewers, they could neither attack nor change it; its disclosure in distraction is therefore of *moral* significance."[72] For Kracauer, the revelation to the masses of ideological fragmentation through the sensory fragmentation, distraction, and superficiality experienced while watching a film is a crucial precondition for the revolution that, as someone influenced at this moment in his life by Jewish Messianism and Marxism, he hopes will bring about a return to the ideological wholeness of premodern times.[73]

Some of Kracauer's interpreters have argued that the shift from the conception of cinema as a technology that reveals truths about social reality in his early film theory to the conception of cinema as revealing truths about physical reality in *Theory of Film* betrays a loss of interest on Kracauer's part or even a repression of the topic of cinema's relation to its historical context. Miriam Hansen, for example, suggests that:

> One might say that history disappears from *Theory of Film* in a double repression: on the level of theory, inasmuch as the specifically modern(ist) moment of film and cinema is transmuted into a medium-specific affinity with physical, external, or visible reality; and, in the same move, on the level of intellectual biography, in that Kracauer seems to have cut himself off completely from his Weimar persona and the radical "love of cinema" that inspired him at the time.[74]

To explore this issue in depth would take me well beyond the scope of this book. But it is worth pointing out that, as we have seen, Kracauer is still concerned with the relation between cinema and its historical context in *Theory of Film*. It is just that his conception of this relation has changed. Whereas in his early film theory Kracauer believed that the cinema would help transform its historical context by revealing the absence of ideological wholeness in modernity through embodying that absence (the lack of ideological wholeness in modernity is embodied in the fragmentary, distracting, superficial sensory experience of cinema), in his later work, he argued that the cinema would help change its historical context by counteracting the cause of the absence of ideological wholeness in modernity (namely, abstractness) and that it would do so by revealing the qualities of objects.

One reason, perhaps, that Kracauer changed his mind about the relationship between the cinema and its historical context as well as his conception of the cinema as a revelatory technology is that, in moving to the United States in the early 1940s, he came into contact with a particularly influential version of the modern subjectivity theory, that of Alfred North Whitehead, whose writings Kracauer refers to and extracts in *Theory of Film*. In works such as *Process and Reality* (1929), Whitehead, the British mathematician and philosopher who taught at Harvard in the 1930s, proposed a new metaphysical theory in response to developments in twentieth-century physics, primarily relativity and quantum theory, which, he believed, had broken up the once stable foundations of science. "The old foundations of scientific thought are becoming unintelligible," Whitehead argued. "Time, space, matter, material, ether, electricity, mechanism, organism, configuration, structure, pattern, function, all require reinterpretation."[75] In place of the metaphysical doctrine of scientific materialism (which, according to Whitehead, dominated the natural sciences from the seventeenth through the end of the nineteenth centuries, and which conceived of reality as consisting of independently existing particles interacting in measurable, predictable ways), Whitehead proposed a new cosmology, which sees a particle "as a vibratory ebb and flow of an underlying energy."[76] Any particular particle consists, according to this theory, of a number of overlapping streams of energy flowing through space and time.

In the 1940s and 1950s, Whitehead's process philosophy, as it was often called, influenced the American avant-garde not unlike how Henri Bergson's philosophy had influenced the European avant-garde several decades earlier. For example, as Daniel Belgrad has argued, painters and poets such as Barnett Newman, Robert Motherwell, and Charles Olson took the concept of the "energy field" from Whitehead in order to justify their art.[77] In *Theory of Film,* the influence of Whitehead's metaphysics can be discerned in Kracauer's talk of "the tremendous energies accumulated in the microscopic configurations of matter," and of reality as an endless continuum. But it is the impact of Whitehead's version of the modern subjectivity theory on Kracauer that particularly concerns us here. One of the social implications of his metaphysics which Whitehead often pointed to is that an organism and its environment are fundamentally continuous because they consist of overlapping streams of energy. And one of the deleterious effects on society of traditional scientific materialism, with its atomistic conception of reality as consisting of separate, individual particles, is that it gives rise to a conception of an organism as separate from its environment, thereby "ignor[ing] . . . the true relation of each organism to its environment [as well as] the intrinsic worth of the environment."[78] Furthermore, the "professionalizing of knowledge" that modern science exemplifies means, Whitehead argued, that in modernity, "there is a development of particular abstractions, and a contraction of concrete appreciation."[79]

The cure for the separation between organism and environment caused by scientific materialism and the highly specialized, abstract education encouraged by modern science lies, Whitehead believed, in aesthetic education broadly conceived. For in the "aesthetic apprehension" of its environment, an organism directly sees and comes into contact with the concrete qualities of the objects around it, rather than separating itself from its environment behind abstractions.

What is wanted is an appreciation of the infinite variety of vivid values achieved by an organism in its proper environment. When you understand all about the sun and all about the atmosphere and all about the rotation of the earth, you may still

miss the radiance of the sunset. There is no substitute for the direct perception of
the concrete achievement of a thing in its actuality. We want concrete fact with a
high light thrown on what is relevant to its preciousness.

What I mean is art and aesthetic education.[80]

Clearly, Whitehead's arguments constitute yet another version of the modern subjectivity theory, at the center of which is the divorce between reality and
subjectivity due to mental abstractions and language and the desire to see "what
the senses have to teach us," to see the world independently of concepts and
words. And, as we have seen, Kracauer makes very similar arguments about
the pernicious abstractness of modernity and the way in which film can coun-
teract this abstractness by revealing the concrete qualities of objects. Whether
or not Kracauer changed his mind about the relationship between cinema and
its historical context, as well as his conception of the cinema as a revelatory
technology, due to Whitehead's influence, it is clear that Kracauer's claims
about the limitations of human vision, like Balázs's, are very much indebted
to the modern subjectivity theory, and that in this respect their visual skepticism differs from that of Epstein and Vertov, who view the flaws of the eye as
innate.

2

The Revelationist Tradition

Critique

I

We have seen how the belief that human vision fails to see the true nature of reality informs the work of Epstein, Vertov, Balázs, and Kracauer, and we have located the immediate sources of this belief. In this chapter I examine more closely the various truths about reality that are revealed by the cinema, according to these theorists, and ask whether the naked eye is really too weak to see them, as they argue.

Due to the influence of Bergson's metaphysics, the most important of these truths for Epstein is mobility, and we have already examined the spatial implications of this concept for his film theory, his claim that the cinema reveals the inner mobile essence or being of objects normally invisible to human sight. The concept of mobility also has temporal implications for Epstein's claims about the cinema's revelatory power. For Bergson, one consequence of the fact that reality is an indivisible, continuous whole is that time is duration, "the continuous progress of the past which gnaws into the future and which swells as it advances."[1] Time does not consist of the replacement of one static, discrete state by another, but rather of one continuous state changing perpetually and unpredictably. Hence, the past is not supplanted by the present and the future, but instead endures into the present and the future, like a "flux of fleeting shades [of color] merging into each other"[2] or the flow of a river. Meanwhile, due to practical necessity, we humans confine ourselves to the present, artificially separating it from the past and the future.

In reality, the past is preserved by itself, automatically. In its entirety, probably, it follows us at every instant; all that we have felt, thought and willed from our earliest infancy is there, leaning over the present which is about to join it, pressing against the portals of consciousness that would fain leave it outside. The cerebral mechanism is arranged just so as to drive back into the unconscious almost the whole of this past, and to admit beyond the threshold only that which can cast light on the present situation or further the action now being prepared—at short only that which can give *useful* work.[3]

Although Bergson here blames "the cerebral mechanism" for confining human beings to the present, he also, as we have seen, attributes a similar flaw to perception, arguing that it "cuts out" objects from their temporal becoming much like a still photograph does. This means that we experience time as a series of static, discrete states, which we then combine together mentally—this is another reason that Bergson claims the human mind is cinematographic.

Epstein is clearly influenced by Bergson's conception of time as duration, and he too claims that humans are confined to the present and are unable to experience time as the flow it really is. However, he tends to blame the *weakness* of our perceptual and cognitive faculties for this, rather than practical necessity.

> Man . . . seems constitutionally unsuited to capture a continuous event in four dimensions all by himself. Man's physiological inability to master the notion of space-time and to escape this atemporal section of the world, which we call the present and of which we are almost exclusively conscious, is the cause of most "accidents of matter and knowing," most of which would be avoided if we could directly seize the world as the flow that it is.[4]

In contrast, the cinema is able to "capture a continuous event in four dimensions."

> But the specific quality of this new projected world [of cinema] is to make another perspective of matter evident, that of time. The fourth dimension, which once seemed mysterious, becomes a notion as banal as that of the other three coordinates through the techniques of slow motion and fast motion. Time is the fourth dimension of a universe of space-time. Cinematography currently is the only instrument that records an event according to a system of four reference points.[5]

Cinema therefore renders the true nature of time as flow or duration visible to the viewer. In the following passage, Epstein is describing close-ups of the human face:

> Even more beautiful than a laugh is the face preparing for it. I must interrupt. I love the mouth which is about to speak and holds back, the gesture which hesitates between right and left, the recoil before the leap, and the moment before landing, the becoming, the hesitation, the taught spring, the prelude, and even more than all these, the piano being tuned before the overture.[6]

The flow of time is revealed in moments of temporal presence—"recoil," "hesitation," "becoming"—in which past and future become visible in the present.

Due to his Bergsonian conception of time, Epstein argues that narrative is antithetical to the cinema because it supposedly divides time into separate states.

> So why tell stories, narratives which always assume a chronology, sequential events, a gradation in facts and feelings? . . . There are no stories. There have never been stories. There are only situations, having neither head nor tail; without beginning, middle, or end, no right side or wrong side; they can be looked at from all directions; right becomes left; without limits in past or future, they are the present.[7]

Narrative, Epstein claims, should therefore be rejected in favor of a "new dramaturgy," which he names an "art of incidences" or "situations." An incident or a situation is a narrative event in which past and future become visible in the present: "Fragments from several pasts take root in a single present. The future erupts through the memories."[8]

In an article about his film *The Three-Sided Mirror* (1927), Epstein indicates that he is attempting to put his theory of the situation into practice. The film tells the story of Him, an unnamed, wealthy businessman who is romantically involved with three women simultaneously. Having abandoned them one day for a ride in the country in his sports car, he crashes after being struck on the forehead by a bird in flight while speeding along a country lane (fig. 2.1). For Epstein, the encounter between Him and the bird is a paradigmatic situation or incidence, because the viewer can see more than the narrative event itself, namely, his past and future and the entire context of the drama in which he has been involved, which crystallizes at the moment the bird strikes him.

> A carefree motorist seems an insignificant character; a swallow in flight even more so; their encounter; the incidence. That little mark which the bird's beak left on the man's forehead had against it the desires of three hearts, the miraculous vigilance of love, all the reflexes of living, all the probabilities in three-dimensional space, every temporal chance. But it took . . . place. In an instant, super saturation produces crystallization. . . . Before and after it, characters and actions suddenly fall obediently into place. In the future, a wrong road unexpectedly intersected in its turn by the ultimate. In the past, viewed enumerated, interlinked, comprehensible, comprehended.[9]

Epstein connects events in the past, present, and future in this film using a radically innovative temporal structure. The film is divided into four numbered sections. In the first three, the three women, one per section, tell somebody nearby about their frustrating, painful love affairs with Him, which the film narrates using elliptical flashbacks. Intercut with these reminiscences are shots of Him retrieving his sports car from a garage and driving through towns from where he sends messages, one at a time, to each of the three women, informing

Figure 2.1. The aftermath of the
crash in *The Three-Sided Mirror*
(Jean Epstein, 1927).

them that he will not be joining them. While the temporal relationship between these shots and the scenes of the women remembering is indeterminate
in sections two and three, the first section strongly implies that they are flash-
forwards. We see Him being driven away from a restaurant where he has just
quarreled with one woman after she has run out of the restaurant and begun
talking about her love affair with Him to a passing stranger. The shots we then
see of Him retrieving his car from the garage, in which he has changed his
clothes, must therefore occur sometime after her reminiscences, which only
take a few minutes. But even if they are occurring roughly simultaneously with
the three women recalling their involvement with Him, they themselves contain
flash-forwards of the road He will drive down to his death, as well as of the telegraph wires on which the bird will perch that will strike Him on the forehead
(figs. 2.2–2.4). Epstein could have strictly adhered to the four-part structure of
the film, confining the scenes of Him in his sports car racing toward his death
to this last section alone, thereby giving each major character in the film their
own section. Instead, he deliberately intercuts these scenes (the future) with
the scenes of the three women reminiscing (the present) about their love affairs
with Him (the past) in an effort to create a strong sense of continuity between
the three temporal dimensions.

That events in the past, present, and future are connected and that the film
medium can represent these connections through flashbacks and flash-forwards
are hardly controversial ideas. But does this mean that humans are confined
to the present due to the weakness of our perceptual and mental faculties? Is
time really something that we could see or experience more of if our eyes were
only stronger, as Epstein claims? This claim suggests that time is like a spatial
whole that we can see more or less of. Just as when we back away from a tall
building we can see more of it, so as we move away from the present we can
see more of the past and future. As Wittgenstein argued in his remarks about
St. Augustine's famous question—What, then, is time?—the surface grammatical analogies in our language between temporal and spatial expressions should
not be taken too far because they mask profound logical differences. For example, there is a surface grammatical analogy between the injunctions "don't
live in the past" and "don't live in Manhattan." But whereas we can ask where

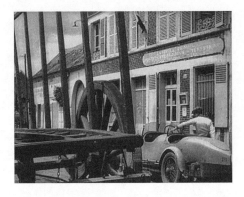

Figure 2.2. A shot of the businessman parking his car outside a telegraph office.

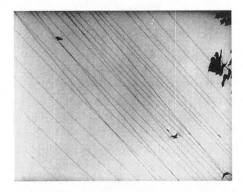

Figure 2.3. Shot in figure 2.2 is followed by a shot of birds perched on telegraph wires.

Figure 2.4. Shot in figure 2.3 is followed by a shot of the businessman leaving the telegraph office with telegram in hand.

Manhattan is and request instructions for getting there, we cannot ask the same of the past.[10]

Augustine takes these surface analogies too far as is evident, according to Wittgenstein, in his discussion of measuring time, his claim that "the past can't be measured, as it is gone by; and the future can't be measured because it has not yet come; and the present can't be measured for it has no extension."[11] Augustine conceives of measuring time as akin to measuring the length of an object, when we are able to see the beginning and end of what we measure.

Because we cannot see the past and the future, we therefore cannot measure time, Augustine concludes. But although there are similarities between measuring time and space, there are also significant logical differences, including the fact that the parts of a temporal whole, unlike the parts of a spatial whole, do not coexist. Hence, it is wrong to demand, as Augustine does, that when measuring time we be able to see the beginning and end of what we measure, for this is to impose the logical grammar of space onto time. Epstein does something similar, conceiving of time as if it were like a spatial whole whose parts (past, present, and future) coexist, but which we are only able to see or experience part of (the present) due to the limitations of our perceptual faculty, as if, were our eyes only stronger, we would be able to see its other parts, too. But whereas we can point to the location of the part of a spatial whole that is out of sight, such as the roof of a tall building, and potentially adjust our position so that we can see it, no matter how strong our eyes are, we cannot point to where events in the past or future are or adjust our position to see them as we should be able to if the past and future did coexist with the present. The present, therefore, is not something we are perceptually confined to due to the limitations of the human eye, in the way that we can be confined to one part of a spatial whole, unable to see its other parts, for confinement implies the possibility of escape, of seeing its other parts as well. And while it is a truism that the cinema is a temporal art that can record events unfolding in time, this does not mean that it enables the viewer to escape the present into the past and future through flashbacks and flash-forwards, thereby making the fourth dimension of time visible, as Epstein suggests. When one sees a flashback in a film, one is not escaping the present and seeing the past. Rather, one is seeing a recording in the present of a past event. To truly escape the present, the cinema would have to enable the viewer to see the flashback when it was shown at the previous night's screening of the film, or when it will be shown at the following night's screening.

Wittgenstein suggested that it is the Augustinian picture of language, the notion that the meaning of a word is the thing named by it, that leads to this confusion about time and many other concepts. Because we use time as a noun, we are easily misled into thinking that it refers to an entity of some kind, which, because we cannot see it, or can only see part of it (the present), must therefore be wholly or in part hidden from us, "something we can see from the outside but which we can't look into."[12] But the dimension of time is not something that we can only see part of, because it is not a thing at all, unlike, say, the spatial dimensions of an object, such as its length or width. This is why we cannot point to its parts or adjust our position to see parts of it better. It is therefore nonsensical to accuse the human eye of failing to see the fourth dimension of time, as Epstein does, and equally nonsensical to argue that the cinema is capable of revealing it.

What about the spatial consequences of the mobile nature of reality? Isn't it true that, whereas from a human perceptual point of view a table, for example, appears still and solid, physical theories have shown that in reality it is mostly empty space in which "sparsely scattered . . . are numerous electric charges rushing about with great speed"?[13] Don't our perceptual faculties create the false impression that reality is static and substantial, as Epstein argues? This is a venerable illusion which Gilbert Ryle attempted to dispel, arguing that there is no genuine rivalry or incompatibility between philosophical and scientific descriptions of the microstructure of objects and our ordinary, everyday perceptual experiences and descriptions of them.[14] This illusion is created, Ryle suggested, by the use of concepts such as "to describe" to cover the disparate goals and activities of the physical theorist and the ordinary person, which "smother" the fundamental differences between them. In fact, argued Ryle, the theorist and the ordinary person are not describing or misdescribing the same things at all, although the former's descriptions presuppose that what the latter is describing exists. First of all, if the theorist describes anything at all, it is the physics of the matter and energy of *all* objects, whereas the ordinary person is typically describing a specific object. Hence, the things about an object described by and of interest to an ordinary person—whether it is a table as opposed to a chair, for example—play no role in the theorist's description, and vice versa. "A bit of the theory of ultimate particles has no place in it for a description or misdescription of chairs and tables, and a description of chairs and tables has no place in it for a description or misdescription of ultimate particles. A statement that is true *or* false of the one is *neither* true *nor* false of the other. It cannot therefore be a rival of the other."[15]

Second, the theorist investigates the microstructure of objects to explain their properties, such as why some things are solids as opposed to gases and liquids. Far from showing that there is no such thing as a solid object, therefore, the theorist is attempting to explain why some things are solids as opposed to gases and liquids, thereby presupposing that there are such things as solids. As P. M. S. Hacker puts it, picking up on Ryle's argument: "If [the theorist] contends that, because my table is a congeries of particles relatively widely separated from each other, therefore it is not (from his point of view) solid, he is in grave conceptual confusion. For it immediately follows that *nothing* on earth *is* solid. So what was he trying to explain?"[16]

If Ryle and Hacker are right, the fact that the microstructure of objects consists of widely separated particles in rapid motion does not show that there are no such things as static, solid objects, as Epstein, like many other moderns, assumes. Indeed, it presupposes the very opposite.

Vertov also assumes that there is a conflict between the world of science and the everyday world, although the science that gives rise to this conflict in his theory is Marxist-Leninism, not physics. In specifying what the cinema reveals about social reality that humans cannot see unaided, Vertov invokes the familiar comparison between the cinema and other visual technologies by asking a rhetorical question about the cinema's difference from microscopes and telescopes, about its unique area of competence: "The eye of the microscope penetrates where the eye of my movie camera cannot. The eye of the telescope reaches distant worlds, inaccessible to my naked eye. What about the camera then? What's its role in my assault on the visible world?"[17] His answer to this question is that the cinema "opens the eyes of the masses to the connection . . . between the social and visual phenomena interpreted by the camera."[18] In other words, the cinema reveals various social relations the eye is too weak to see between the phenomena it can see.

A major example of the revelation of such relations occurs, Annette Michelson has argued, in Vertov's 1924 film *Kinoglaz*.

> We first see a peasant woman on her way to the market to buy meat. We next see her, walking backwards, propelled by the reversal of that sequence, whence she came. The processing and distribution of meats is then recapitulated in reverse, as well. . . . And later in the film, from a Pioneer's diary, [intertitle number] 64: "If time went backwards the bread would return to the bakery." And the film then continues with a recapitulation of bread distribution and manufacture.[19]

According to Michelson, in this film Vertov uses reverse motion to go back in time and reveal, in Vertov's own words, "the origins of objects" such as bread and meat, origins that the human eye is too weak to see because of its temporal immobility, its confinement to the present.[20] Such a revelation, argues Vertov, has a potentially transformative impact on workers in his audience because it undoes what Marxists call "commodity fetishism," making "it possible for every worker to acquire, through evidence, the conviction that he, the worker, creates all these [objects] himself, and that consequently they belong to him."[21] Thus, the social relation that this sequence supposedly reveals is one between the worker purchasing the meat in the present and the various workers producing it in the past.

In general, as Michelson has shown, what Vertov attempts to reveal in his films are the various social relations—putatively invisible to the naked human eye—that, as a Marxist, he believes connect citizens of the new Soviet republics: relations of economic interdependency between town and city, between different types of labor and sectors of the economy, between different ethnicities, regions, and nationalities within the Soviet Union, and so on. *Man with a Movie Camera,* for example,

> joins the human life cycle with the cycles of work and leisure of a city from dawn to dusk within the spectrum of industrial production. That production includes filmmaking (itself presented as a range of productive labor processes), mining, steel production, communications, postal service, construction, hydro-electric power installation, and the textile industry in a seamless, organic continuum.[22]

Vertov reveals these social relations to demonstrate to Soviet citizens that they are part of a new, general community in which they are all equally interdependent and all equally owners of the means of production, thereby furthering the Marxist project of overcoming the alienation of private property in capitalism.[23] And he does this by exploiting the two ways he believes the cinema is superior to human vision: its mobility, its capacity to move rapidly through space and time between citizens engaged in different activities in different places at different times throughout the Soviet Union; and the precision of editing, which allows him to link these disparate subjects into intelligible patterns.[24]

As with connections between events in the past, present, and future, it is hardly controversial to say that people are connected in the sense of being linked by various social relations and that the cinema can represent these relations. But does this license Vertov's claim that such social relations are invisible to the naked eye, as if, were our eyes more powerful, we would be able to see them? Once again Ryle comes to the rescue with some perspicuous analogies. In some card games, for example, cards in a certain suit are designated trumps by the rules of the game. But this does not mean that being a trump is some "occult or latent [property] behind the glossy faces of the cards."[25] Similarly, the price of a commodity is not "an invisible quality of the thing, whose detection requires some mysterious super-perceptive faculties."[26] In both cases, the fact that we say that being a trump or having a price is a property or attribute of the card or commodity in question can mislead us into thinking that they are like intrinsic physical properties we can see and describe, such as that a card has a rectangular shape. Because the property of being a trump, unlike having a rectangular shape, is not visible, we therefore assume it must be invisible in the sense that our eyes are not powerful enough to see it, much like its particulate structure is. But, of course, that a particular card is a trump is not an intrinsic physical property of the card like its particulate structure, but rather a property it possesses by virtue of its interaction with other cards as defined by the rules of the game being played. Similarly, the price of a commodity is determined by its interaction with other commodities and the market conditions in which it is made and consumed. It is not an intrinsic physical property of the commodity like its mass. Hence, it is to these interactions, and the contexts in which they occur, that we turn if we want to find out whether a card is a trump or if we want to know the price of a commodity. No matter how powerful our eyes might be, we would not be able to see that a card is a trump or know the price of the commodity just by looking at them in isolation from these interactions and contexts. Furthermore, we are able to perceive these interactions without the help of a visual technology. Unless we are suffering from a perceptual or cognitive impairment, we are capable of discovering the rules of a card game by watching the game being played and determining that a particular card is a trump, unaided, just as we can find out about market conditions, view a commodity being produced and consumed, and figure out its price without assistance.

The same is true of social relations, such as marriage or the relation of consumer to producer. Being married is not like an intrinsic physical property we are incapable of seeing unaided, nor is being a consumer. Instead, the relation of marriage is created through a specific type of interaction, namely, the act of marrying, and one becomes a consumer through another type of interaction, the act of consumption. If we want to discover these relations, we must consult records of these interactions, such as marriage certificates and receipts of purchase, or witnesses to them, which we are quite able to do without a visual technology. Ditto the social relations that Vertov endeavors to inform his viewers of in his films. That a commodity is produced in the country and consumed in the city and that the city is, therefore, dependent on the country for this commodity is determined by the various interactions that constitute the market conditions in which the commodity is made and purchased—that the raw materials used to make the commodity originate in the country, that it is cheaper to buy it from the country, and so on—which we must investigate if we want to find out where it comes from and why. This is precisely, of course, what Vertov does in his films, despite what he claims in his theory. When showing us the origins of meat in *Kinoglaz,* he is not revealing something our eyes are not powerful enough to see in the same way that a microscope could reveal the meat's particulate structure. Instead, he is informing us of certain facts about the market conditions in which the meat is sold by depicting the interactions that constitute these market conditions, such as the slaughter of the cow in the slaughterhouse. Vertov in effect hypostatizes social relations in his film theory, conceiving of them as if they were physical, intrinsic properties of things that the eye is incapable of seeing unaided, when in fact they are properties things possess by virtue of their interactions with the world, interactions we are in many instances perfectly capable of perceiving or finding out about without assistance. It is therefore as nonsensical to accuse the eye of failing to see these social relations as it is to accuse it of failing to see the past and the future.

What about Vertov's claim that our perceptions are disorganized and confusing? Does this make sense? No, because although psychologists talk of "having perceptions," this does not mean that seeing consists of separate perceptions joined together in the way that a film consists of separate shots that are edited together. We cannot count our perceptions, whereas we can count the number of shots in a film. Nor can we ask whether we had a perception today or yesterday, whereas we can ask whether a shot was filmed today or yesterday. Hence, our perceptions cannot be badly organized, in the way that a film can be badly edited, for there are no separate things to organize. Instead, *what* we see is confusing or badly organized (which also means that it can be clear and well organized, like a formal garden), or it is seen today or yesterday. This is why we do not say that we see something confusedly, or that our seeing of it is confused. Rather, we say that we are confused *by what* we see, or we say that *what* we see is confusing, because it is what we see that can confuse us, not our act of seeing it. Nor does Vertov's talk of the cinema being more mobile than the human eye, of being "free of the limits of time and space," make sense. If a film camera is not present to record an event as it happens, it cannot go backward or forward in time to record it. Nor can it move instantaneously between one place and another to record events, for it has to be taken between places to do so, usually by human beings, which takes time. It is the change from one shot to another in a film that can be instantaneous (or not). But this does not mean that the viewer is suddenly transported from one place and time to another when the shot changes, for the viewer remains in the same place (the movie theater) and time (the present) throughout. Rather, it means that there is an instantaneous transition between shots recorded at different places and times. Vertov systematically conflates the instantaneous transition between shots recorded at different times and places with the act of recording them to make it seem as if the camera itself can move instantaneously between different times and places and is therefore more mobile than the human eye.

Time and social relations are good examples of the first type of truth about reality found in the revelationist tradition. These relations are things that the eye cannot intelligibly be accused of failing to see because they are not the sort of things than can be seen. Emotion and family resemblance, which are found in Epstein's film theory, are examples of the second: things that it is logically and empirically possible for human beings to see unaided.

For Epstein, the cinema reveals the inner mental life of human beings, in particular their feelings. "The close-up is drama in high gear. A man says, 'I love the faraway princess.' Here the verbal gearing down is suppressed. I can see love. It half lowers its eyelids, raises the arc of the eyebrows laterally, inscribes itself on the taut forehead, swells the masseters, hardens the tuft of the chin, flickers on the mouth and at the edge of the nostrils."[27] When a face is filmed in close-up, Epstein is claiming, the viewer can see more than the external material surface or properties of the face in question, namely, inner feelings ("I can see love"), as if, like the particulate structure of an object, the naked eye is normally not strong enough to see such feelings. Indeed, Epstein looks forward to a time when the movie camera will be used as a device for revealing to prospective lovers their partners' emotions: "Possibilities are already appearing for the drama of the microscope, a hystophysiology *[sic]* of the passions, a classification of the amorous sentiments. . . . Young girls will consult them instead of the fortune teller."[28]

The argument that the cinema reveals the inner mental life of human beings is also made by other film theorists during this period, including Balázs, and I will examine Balázs's version of it later in this chapter. Somewhat unique to Epstein's version is that he extends this argument beyond the human face and body to include material objects. For Epstein, not only does the cinema uncover the interior life of human beings, it also reveals the interior life of objects.

> A close-up of a revolver is no longer a revolver, it is the revolver-character, in other words the impulse towards or remorse for crime, failure, suicide. It is as dark as the temptations of the night, bright as the gleam of gold lusted after, taciturn as passion, squat, brutal, heavy, cold, wary, menacing. It has a temperament, habits, memories, a will, a soul.[29]

Epstein refers to the interior life of an object as its "personality," which he defines partly in Bergsonian terms: "Personality is the spirit visible in things and people, their heredity made evident, their past become unforgettable, their future already present."[30] When the personality of an object is revealed by the movie camera, the viewer can see more than an inert, material object. The object seems to come alive, as if it were a living being of some kind.

> Through the cinema, a revolver in a drawer, a broken bottle on the ground, an eye isolated by an iris, are elevated to the status of characters in the drama. Being dramatic, they seem alive, as though involved in the evolution of an emotion. . . . To things and beings in their most frigid semblance, the cinema thus grants the greatest gift unto death: life. And it confers this life in its highest guise: personality.[31]

So great is the power of the cinema to reveal personality that it can make an
entire environment of objects appear alive:

> True tragedy remains in abeyance. It threatens all the faces. It is in the curtain at
> the window and the handle of the door. Each drop of ink can make it bloom on
> the tip of the fountain pen. In the glass of water it dissolves. The whole room is
> saturated with every kind of drama. The cigar smoke is poised menacingly over the
> ashtray's throat. The dust is treacherous. The carpet emits venomous arabesques
> and the arms of the chair tremble.[32]

At first sight, the argument that the cinema reveals the personality of an
object may appear very mysterious. However, Epstein demystifies it somewhat
by invoking the experience of possessing a personal object:

> Each of us, I assume, must possess some object which he holds onto for personal
> reasons: for some it's a book; for some, perhaps, a very banal and somewhat
> ugly trinket; for someone else, perhaps, a piece of furniture with no value. We
> do not look at them as they really are. To tell the truth, we are incapable of see-
> ing them as objects. What we see in them, through them, are the memories and
> emotions, the plans or regrets that we have attached to these things for a more or
> less lengthy period of time, sometimes forever. Now, this is the cinematographic
> mystery: an object such as this, with its personal character, that is to say, an
> object situated in a dramatic action that is equally photographic in character, re-
> veals anew its moral character, its human and living expression when reproduced
> cinematographically.[33]

Just as a personal object can sometimes seem to come alive with the various "memories and emotions" with which it is associated to the owner who is
looking at it, so an object filmed in close-up can seem to come alive with the
various narrative elements with which it is associated to the viewer looking at
it. Epstein provides a simple cinematic example to illustrate this point:

> I imagine a banker receiving bad news at home from the stock exchange. He is
> about to telephone. The call is delayed. Close-up of the telephone. If the shot of
> the telephone is shown clearly, if it is well-written, you no longer see a mere tele-
> phone. You read: ruin, failure, misery, prison, suicide. And in other circumstances,
> this same telephone will say: sickness, doctor, help, death, solitude, grief. And at
> yet another time this same telephone will cry gaily: joy, love, liberty. All this may
> seem extremely simple; they may be regarded as childish symbols. I confess that it
> seems very mysterious to me that one can in this way charge the simple reflection
> of inert objects with an intensified sense of life, that one can animate it with its
> own vital import.[34]

Epstein is arguing that the cinema reveals the interior life or personality of an
object in the sense that the close-up can animate an object with the context of
the narrative within which it is embedded.

Another phenomenon that Epstein argues is revealed by the cinema is family resemblance. In the following passage, he talks about his experience of watching a home movie depicting two generations of a single family.

> From oldest ancestor to youngest child, all the resemblances and differences delineated a single character. The family seemed to me like an individual whose dissimilar members never disrupted the sense of unity and, on the contrary, proved necessary to its equilibrium. . . . Not a single person in the assembled group seemed to me free, neither in what they had been, nor in what they were, nor in what they would be. And what issued from the mouth of one or another was the family, which answered me with its singular voice, according to its singular character, with its set way of thinking and which carried on across many past, present, and future bodies.[35]

Here, Epstein describes family resemblance as if it were an invisible, immaterial, almost platonic entity existing independently of each family member. It is only the cinema, according to Epstein, that has the power to capture this strange entity, to render it visible to the film viewer through the accumulation of images of the family across time. "Once cinematography will have reached the century mark of its existence . . . it will have been able to capture the startling and instructive appearances of this familial monster. Many other concepts await their personification through cinematography; among the closest are heredity, the affectations of the mind, diseases."[36]

Once again, as with emotion, the revelation of family resemblance by the movie camera involves the viewer seeing more than the external material surface of the feature of reality being depicted in the cinematic image—namely, the "familial monster" that lurks in each family member, waiting to be revealed or personified by the cinema.

What is important about emotion and family resemblance is that, unlike time and "the relations of workers with each other," they are phenomena that it makes perfect sense to say that we see, as Wittgenstein pointed out in his investigation into an unusual visual experience he called "aspect-dawning" in section xi of part 2 of *Philosophical Investigations*. Although the duck-rabbit provides the most famous example of this experience, Wittgenstein gives many others: "I suddenly see the solution of a picture-puzzle. Before, there were branches there; now there is a human shape. My visual impression has changed and now I recognize that it has not only shape and color but also a quite particular 'organization.'"[37] What makes aspect-dawning an unusual visual experience is that, like some of the truths revealed by the cinema according to Epstein, it appears to involve the beholder "seeing" more than the material properties of the object he is looking at. This is because the object of sight remains materially unchanged during aspect-dawning. Nothing is physically added to or taken away from it to change its appearance. Yet, once the aspect has dawned, the beholder seems to see something different about the object—what Wittgenstein calls an aspect—even though he knows there is nothing new to see about it, materially speaking. Thus, as Wittgenstein points out, an "exact copy" of the object of sight before the dawning of an aspect will be identical to an exact copy of it once the aspect has dawned because, materially, the object remains the same. Hence, the beholder's claim that he sees something new about an object during aspect-dawning can seem paradoxical and confusing. Wittgenstein sums up this sense of paradox in the following way: "The change of aspect. 'But surely you would say that the picture is altogether different now!' But what is different: my impression? my point of view?—Can I say? I *describe* the alteration like a perception; quite as if the object had altered before my eyes" (PI 195; emphasis in original).

Wittgenstein includes family resemblance and emotion—phenomena that Epstein argues are revealed by the cinema—under the concept of an aspect because they occasion familiar examples of aspect-dawning. They can suddenly be "seen" in a face without the material properties of the face in question changing. Indeed, Wittgenstein's first example of aspect-dawning in section xi is the resemblance between two faces: "I contemplate a face, and then suddenly notice its likeness to another. I *see* that it has not changed; and yet I see it differently" (PI 193; emphasis in original). Likeness cannot, therefore, be represented using an exact copy or an accurate drawing of the faces in question, although it can be seen in a drawing of the faces: "The one man might make an accurate drawing of the two faces, and the other notice in the drawing the likeness which the former did not see" (PI 193). Similarly, an emotion expressed in a face, such as friendliness, is something that a beholder may suddenly see, even though the material properties of the face remain unchanged (PI 199). Wittgenstein also gives as an example of aspect-dawning, or at least something very similar to aspect-dawning, the curious experience that Epstein refers to as the revelation of the personality of an object in which an object seems to come alive to the beholder. This experience is very similar to aspect-dawning, because during it the beholder behaves as if the object looked different to him, as if it had changed in some way, even though the beholder knows that it has not. For example, the beholder describes the object differently. "I might say: a picture does not always *live* for me while I am seeing it. 'Her picture smiles down on me from the wall.' It need not always do so, whenever my glance lights on it" (PI 205; emphasis in original).

In the first part of section xi of the *Investigations,* Wittgenstein tries to dissolve the air of paradox and confusion that can surround aspect-dawning. He does so by investigating the meaning of the concept of seeing, when and how it is employed correctly, to clarify precisely what the beholder means when he says that he sees something new about an object during aspect-dawning. "But this isn't *seeing!*" insists one of Wittgenstein's imaginary interlocutors. "But this is seeing!" demands another. Wittgenstein replies: "It must be possible to give both remarks a conceptual justification. But this is seeing! *In what sense* is it seeing?" (PI 203; emphasis in original). Wittgenstein's detailed answer to this question, which requires some careful unpacking, demonstrates that the widespread assumption that we can only see the material properties of things is false. In Epstein's theory, this erroneous assumption in combination with the Romantic theory of intuition gives rise to the claim that the cinema reveals emotion and family resemblance, which the naked eye cannot see because it is confined to the external material properties of objects.

To answer the question of what sense seeing an aspect is seeing, Wittgenstein attempts to unearth the relevant criteria that govern correct uses of the concept of seeing. As usual, to avoid the charge that he is inventing these criteria or that they are not verifiable, he examines situations in which they are most visible: standard, third-person uses of the concept. According to Wittgenstein, the criteria governing the correct use of any concept cannot be private, hidden, or unknown, awaiting discovery by the philosopher. If they were, the concept would be unusable and unteachable. Hence, the criteria governing correct uses of the concept of seeing must lie in public, observable, verbal and nonverbal behavior in context. P. M. S. Hacker summarizes this element of Wittgenstein's argument in the following way:

> That a creature can perceive is established by observing its behavior, its discriminatory, conative and affective responses to visibilia, audibilia, etc., its use of its perceptual organs in discerning objects, sounds, smells or warmth in its environment. It is not the eye, brain, mind or soul that perceives, but . . . the living creature; and we determine *that* it perceives by observing its *behavior* in appropriate circumstances.[38]

What are the criteria for saying that somebody sees something? To answer this question, Wittgenstein imagines examples in which a hypothetical beholder is asked to report on what he sees when shown a variety of standard images and objects instead of ones that occasion unusual visual experiences such as aspect-dawning. One obvious criterion for saying that the beholder sees what he is shown is that he will, when asked, identify the kind of object he is shown correctly. However, Wittgenstein points out that this is not a sufficient criterion for saying that the beholder actually sees what he is shown. "I see that an animal in a picture is transfixed by an arrow. It has struck it in the throat and sticks out at the back of the neck. Let the picture be a silhouette.—Do you *see* the arrow—or do you merely *know* that these two bits are supposed to represent part of an arrow? (Compare Köhler's figure of the interpenetrating hexagons.)" (PI 203; emphasis in original.)

Somebody who cannot see the animal transfixed by the arrow in this schematic figure (a silhouette) may well be able to infer what the figure depicts from the spatial arrangement of the lines ("two bits") and other clues, and therefore identify the kind of object the figure depicts correctly. What, therefore, are the criteria for saying that somebody actually sees the animal transfixed by the arrow in this figure, as opposed to merely knowing or inferring what the figure depicts? According to Wittgenstein, these criteria lie in the way the beholder makes his report about what the figure depicts, and the precise form of words he uses.

First, somebody who sees the animal transfixed by the arrow will be able to offer his report about the kind of object depicted in the figure immediately on being shown it (given conditions in which his sense of sight is not impaired for some reason—for example, by insufficient light). He will spontaneously and unhesitatingly respond to a question about what he sees with a correct report about the kind of object the figure depicts, even if he is shown the figure only for a few seconds (PI 203–204). Meanwhile, somebody who does not see the animal transfixed by an arrow will not, on being shown the figure, be able to respond immediately. Rather, such a person will need a period of time to infer what kind of object the spatial arrangement of the lines in the figure is supposed to represent, and he may well make an incorrect inference. In his verbal report, he will probably make reference to these lines, saying something like, "These lines represent . . ."

Second, if a beholder is not able to see the animal transfixed by the arrow, he has to infer what the figure is supposed to depict, and inference-making by definition involves considering a number of interpretations to find the most plausible one. Hence, in his verbal report, he may well say something like, "These lines could represent an arrow, or they could represent a spear, or they could represent something else long and pointed." Meanwhile, somebody who sees the arrow will not consider a variety of interpretations, because, if he is describing what he sees truthfully and accurately, his report that he sees the arrow is the only one he can give. A beholder will not consider a variety of interpretations of the lines if he sees an arrow in them, because no interpretation is needed. As Wittgenstein puts it, "But I cannot try to see a conventional picture of a lion *as* a lion, any more than an F as that letter" (PI 206; emphasis in original).

What does an example such as this one teach us about the concept of seeing? First, it shows that it is the way that a beholder behaves, his particular attitude, that constitutes one of the criteria for saying that he sees the kind of object something is. "'To me it is an animal pierced by an arrow.' That is what I treat it as; this is my *attitude* to the figure. This is one meaning in calling it a case of 'seeing'" (PI 205; emphasis in original). A beholder who sees the animal transfixed by the arrow in the schematic figure will not only identify what he is shown correctly, but will identify it in a particular manner: he will spontaneously and unhesitatingly report what kind of object is depicted in the figure, and he will not treat his identification as one among several possible interpretations of the figure. His reaction will be as automatic and unthinking as chewing when eating: "One doesn't '*take*' what one knows as the cutlery at a meal *for* cutlery; any more than one ordinarily tries to move one's mouth as one eats, or aims at moving it" (PI 195; emphasis in original).

Second, this example demonstrates that we apply the concept of seeing to two different "objects of sight" (PI 193). "If I saw the duck-rabbit as a rabbit, then I saw: these shapes and colors (I give them in detail)—and I saw besides something like this: and here I point to a number of different pictures of rabbits.—This shews the difference between the concepts" (PI 196–197). The first object of sight is material properties such as shape and color. These can be pointed to, described, and represented using an exact copy. The second object of sight is the kind of object something is, in this case a rabbit depicted in a picture. The difference between the two types of object of sight is evident in the way they are represented by the beholder. Unlike material properties, the "rab-bitness" of the rabbit in the picture, its *identity* as a rabbit, what Wittgenstein calls its aspect, cannot be pointed to, described, or represented using an exact copy. Instead, it can only be represented by pointing to other pictures that also depict rabbits. In the case of the schematic figure of the animal transfixed by an arrow, both beholders see the first type of object of sight—namely, the material properties of the figure. They can, for example, describe the spatial arrangement of its lines. But only one of the beholders can see the second type of object of sight—the kind of object depicted in the figure.

A simple thought experiment might help clarify the difference between these two objects of sight. Let us imagine that a tribe of English-speaking peo-ple, who do not use cutlery or have any concept of cutlery, and who have never seen or heard of cutlery, is discovered in a remote corner of Wisconsin. One of them is shown a fork and asked what it is that he sees. He describes the material features of the fork perfectly: its color, shape, texture, and so on. But would we say that he sees a fork? In one sense we would, for he describes its mate-rial properties very well. But in another sense we wouldn't. He does not see a fork, but just an object with a certain color, shape, and texture. It is this other sense of the concept of seeing—seeing the kind of object something is, not just its material properties—that Wittgenstein is trying to clarify in section xi of *Investigations*.

Third, this example shows that we speak of seeing both objects of sight in the domain of images. The fact that humans identify the kind of objects de-picted in images spontaneously and unhesitatingly, and the fact that they do not treat their identifications as one among several possible interpretations, consti-tute grounds for saying that they see the kind of objects depicted in images. They do not just see the material properties of images—their surface shapes and colors—and then infer what kind of objects these images are supposed to represent. Wittgenstein calls seeing the kind of object depicted in an image "continuous seeing of an aspect," or "regarding-as" (PI 205).

Section xi of *Investigations* does not contain a complete investigation of the concept of seeing, and it leaves many questions unanswered. Its purpose, instead, is to clarify the concept of seeing sufficiently enough to dissolve the paradox and confusion that surround aspect-dawning. The fact that seeing has at least two distinct objects of sight explains why the unusual visual experience of aspect-dawning can seem paradoxical and confusing. Aspect-dawning is an unusual visual experience because it foregrounds this distinction. Normally, when we see an object with which we are familiar, whether in reality or de-picted in an image, we can see what kind of object it is at the same time that we see its material properties. As Wittgenstein puts it in relation to images, "The aspects in a change of aspects are those ones which the figure might some-times have *permanently* in a picture" (PI 201; emphasis in original). However, in aspect-dawning seeing the kind of object that something is is delayed. In the case of images that occasion aspect-dawning, for example, either we see one kind of object the material properties of the image depict, and then notice that these same material properties can be seen as another, very different, kind of object, as in the duck-rabbit, or we see the material properties of the image first, such as the lines in the picture puzzle, and then see what kind of object those material properties depict, such as the human shape.

If one understands the object of sight in the first sense mentioned above (seeing material properties), then the beholder's claim that he can see something new about the object once the aspect has dawned seems paradoxical and confusing. In this first sense, as the imaginary interlocutor insists, aspect-dawning is not seeing. But if one understands the object of sight in the second sense, as seeing the kind of object something is, then there is nothing paradoxical or confusing about the beholder's claim. Aspect-dawning does involve seeing something new in the second sense, because what one sees when an aspect dawns is the kind of object something is.

We can now finally return to the question of why it makes sense to say that we see family resemblance and emotion, phenomena that Epstein argues cannot be seen with the naked human eye but can only be revealed by the cinema. "'We *see* emotion'—As opposed to what?—We do not see facial contortions and *make the inference* that he is feeling joy, grief, boredom. We describe the face immediately as sad, radiant, bored, even when we are unable to give any other description of the features.—Grief, one would like to say, is personified in the face. This is essential to what we call 'emotion.'"[39]

We say that human beings see emotion in a face, as opposed to merely seeing the material features of a face and inferring what emotion its owner is feeling, because of their verbal and nonverbal behavior. Humans can spontaneously and unhesitatingly identify a face as sad, happy, and so on, without treating their identification as one among several possible interpretations. Similarly, we say that people see family resemblance because, again, they can immediately identify that a face is like another face without saying, for example, "The shape of his nose suggests that he could belong to the Smith family, but the color of his hair and eyes suggests that he could be a member of the Jones clan."

The curious experience that Epstein refers to as the revelation of the personality of an object, in which an object seems to come alive to the beholder, is a somewhat more complex phenomenon. To do justice to it fully would require a much more in-depth examination of Wittgenstein's remarks about aspect-dawning than I have given. Since such an examination is beyond the scope of this book, and since others have attempted it, I will only suggest in what sense we "see" the emotional life of an object.[40]

According to Wittgenstein, there are other behavioral grounds for "regarding-as"—for saying that humans see the kind of objects depicted in images, their aspects, and not just their material properties—beyond the criteria examined above. These include the larger role that images play in human life: "You need to think of the role which pictures such as paintings (as opposed to working drawings) have in our lives" (PI 205). For as Wittgenstein points out, in certain ways, we treat an image as we do the object it depicts. "In some respects I stand towards [a picture-face] as I do towards a human face. I can study its expression, can react to it as to the expression of the human face. A child can talk to picture-men or picture-animals, can treat them as it treats dolls" (PI 194). For example, at certain moments we treat an image as if it had become the object it depicts, as if it were the living embodiment of that object. People often revere images of loved ones, for instance, hanging them on a wall or keeping them in a special place. And sometimes, such an image is treated as if it were the loved one. It is taken down from the wall, kissed, stroked, and talked to. Wittgenstein refers to such moments as examples of "seeing-as," not regarding-as.

> The question is whether yet another concept, related to [regarding-as], is also of importance to us: that, namely, of a seeing-as which only takes place while I am actually concerning myself with the picture as the object depicted.
>
> I might say: a picture does not always *live* for me while I am seeing it. "Her picture smiles down on me from the wall." It need not always do so, whenever my glance lights on it.
>
> The duck-rabbit. One asks oneself: how can the eye—this *dot*—be looking in a direction?—"*See, it is looking!*" (And one "looks" oneself as one says this.) But one does not say and do this the whole time one is looking at the picture. (PI 205; emphasis in original.)

For Wittgenstein, the experience of "seeing-as," in which an image seems alive for a short period of time because it appears to become the object it depicts, is to be distinguished from regarding-as because, during "seeing-as," the beholder is intensely preoccupied or concerned with the kind of object an image depicts, with its aspect, whereas during regarding-as he isn't. A beholder may always regard an image as the object it depicts, but only sometimes, if at all, become preoccupied with its aspect to the extent that he experiences seeing-as. However, seeing-as constitutes an important behavioral criterion for regarding-as, for saying that human beings see the kind of object an image depicts. For if we could only see the material properties of images and had to infer what images are supposed to depict, we would not be able to experience seeing-as. We would not, in other words, be able to experience moments in which an image seems to become the object it depicts because we would not be able to *see* the object in the image. We would not, therefore, treat images of, say, loved ones in the way that we do, nor would we treat images as the objects they depict in other ways. We would not, to use Wittgenstein's example of the picture face, "study its expression" or "react to it as to the expression of the human face." The role that images play in our lives would be very different.

The most important thing about what Wittgenstein calls seeing-as here is that it can be experienced in relation to nonmimetic representations, as shown by the way human beings treat such representations. For example, not only do we revere images of loved ones. We also revere letters written by them, or objects that belong to them. And sometimes, we behave toward these nonmimetic representations as if they had become the living embodiment of what they represent. As Epstein points out, for example, what is for someone else a "banal and somewhat ugly trinket" may, at certain moments, seem to us to incarnate the "memories and emotions, the plans or regrets that we have attached to these things." Hence, just as with an image of the loved one, we may kiss, stroke, and even talk to the trinket. Nor is such an experience confined to *personal* nonmimetic representations. In religious practices, for example, certain objects—one thinks of relics and the sacrament in the Christian religion—are treated as if they were the living embodiment of the divine. And in aesthetic experiences, as Wittgenstein pointed out, we often behave toward art works as if they had become what they represent:

> But the expression in one's voice and gestures is the same as if the object had altered and had ended by *becoming* this or that.
>
> I have a theme played to me several times and each time in a slower tempo. In the end I say "*Now* it's right," or "*Now* at last it's a march," "*Now* at last it's a dance."—The same tone of voice expresses the dawning of an aspect. (PI 206; emphasis in original.)

In what sense does the experience of "seeing as" in which an object seems to come alive—what Epstein refers to as the revelation of the personality of an object—involve seeing? Clearly, the use of the concept of seeing in the context of this experience involves an extension of the concept. Unlike the experience of aspect-dawning, in which the beholder suddenly notices the kind of object an image depicts (the face in the lines of the picture puzzle, for example), there is nothing new to see about an image or a nonmimetic representation when it seems to become the living embodiment of what it represents. Nevertheless, as Wittgenstein points out in the above quotation, during "seeing-as," the beholder behaves in a manner strongly analogous to the way he behaves during aspect-dawning. For example, he behaves "as if the object had altered and had ended by *becoming* this or that" (PI 206; emphasis in original), just as, during aspect-dawning, he describes "the alteration like a perception; quite as if the object had altered before [his] eyes" (PI 195). The beholder, in other words, reacts toward and describes the object as if something had changed about it, as if it looked different to him, even though he knows that nothing has changed about it materially, just as he does during aspect-dawning. To use Epstein's example of the personal trinket again, the owner of the trinket behaves toward it as if he sees something different about it than the beholder for whom the trinket has no personal value, as if it looked different to him. It is for this reason, I suggest, that we are inclined to use the concept of seeing to describe this curious experience (and indeed why Wittgenstein calls it "seeing-as"), even if we use it in an extended sense. A beholder for whom an object appears alive with emotion behaves as if he can see something different about the object, as if it looks different to him, just as he does during aspect-dawning. Hence, we are inclined to say that he "sees" something about it that others do not.

If Wittgenstein is right, therefore, two of the three phenomena at the core of Epstein's theory of the cinema's revelatory power—emotion and family resemblance—can be seen, logically speaking, by us. What Wittgenstein, of course, makes no mention of is the need for visual technologies to see these phenomena. This is because, contrary to Epstein's theory, human beings standardly can and do see, unaided, the resemblance between two faces, see emotions manifested in other peoples' faces, and undergo the curious experience in which objects, such as objects belonging to loved ones, come alive for them. The naked human eye, unless it is suffering from a visual impairment, is not too weak to see these things, as Epstein claims. It is not confined to the external material properties of things and people. Like his arguments about the invisibility of the fourth dimension of time and Vertov's arguments about the invisibility of social relations, Epstein is only able to make this claim about the limitations of human vision and the revelatory power of the cinema through a misuse of perceptual concepts.

II

We have seen that Epstein and Vertov confuse things that it is logically impossible for human beings to see with things the eye is not strong enough to see. In addition, Epstein denies vision the capacity to see things that it can see perfectly well unaided. The truths about reality revealed by the cinema in Balázs and Kracauer's theories are, on the whole, of the latter kind. Indeed, in Balázs's theory, we find two of the same truths that we encountered in Epstein's. Because it isolates and magnifies details, Balázs, like Epstein, argues that the close-up reveals the inner life of objects, which he often refers to as the "face of objects." And, again like Epstein, Balázs claims that the interior life that objects seem to possess when filmed in close-up is derived from the various narrative elements with which they are associated, principally the emotions of characters.

> When the film close-up strips the veil of our imperceptiveness and insensitivity from the hidden little things and shows us the face of objects, it still shows us man, for what makes objects expressive are the human expressions projected onto them. The objects only reflect our own selves. . . . When we see the face of things, we do what the ancients did in creating *gods* in man's image and breathing a human soul into them. The close-ups of the film are the creative instruments of this highly visual anthropomorphism.[41]

For Balázs, however, the most important thing revealed by the close-up is the inner mental life of human beings, and Balázs calls the capacity of the close-up to reveal this inner mental life "microphysiognomics."

Balázs provides numerous examples of microphysiognomics in action. For instance, as we saw in the example of the duplicitous priest in the Introduction, the close-up can uncover the truth in a liar's face: "However disciplined and practisedly hypocritical a face may be, in the enlarging close-up we see even that it is concealing something, that it is looking a lie" (TTF 63). It can do this by revealing whether facial movements are natural: "The microscopic close-up is an inexorable censor of 'naturalness' of expression; it immediately shows up the difference between spontaneous reaction and deliberate, unnatural, forced gesture" (TTF 77). The majority of Balázs's examples of microphysiognomics, however, concern the revelation of emotions expressed in the details of faces and bodies that the naked eye could not, he argues, see unaided: "Close-ups are often dramatic revelations of what is really happening under the surface of appearances. You may see a medium shot of someone sitting and conducting a conversation with icy calm. The close-up will show trembling fingers nervously fumbling a small object—sign of an internal storm" (TTF 56).

As we saw in chapter 1, Balázs argues that the cinema is needed to reveal inner emotions in the details of behavior in part because human beings have forgotten how to express their emotions using their bodies, and hence have forgotten how to see the body as expressive of mind. But does this make sense? Can emotions exist permanently "unexpressed" or "submerged," to use Balázs's words? This argument conceives of outer behavior as independent of inner mental life, something that can be dispensed with or "forgotten," as if it is superfluous to the inner mind, as if the mind were intrinsically private and could exist independently of the outer. But according to Wittgenstein in his criticisms of similar arguments found in the Cartesian tradition, what we call inner mental life is logically dependent on outer behavior. In the absence of the outer, our concepts of the inner would become unusable and meaningless. Wittgenstein attempts to show this in his so-called private language arguments.

If inner phenomena such as sensations occurred in an internal, private world, then learning the correct concept to refer to a sensation—say the concept "pain" to refer to the sensation of pain—would consist of associating the concept with a sensation that only the language learner can feel and know to be present or not. But this would render the concept unintelligible, according to Wittgenstein, and he shows this in at least two ways. First, others would never be able to know whether or not the concept for the sensation was being used correctly by the language learner. Such a sensation would be like something hidden in a box—say, a beetle—that only its owner can look into (PI §293). Because the object in each person's box can be seen and known only to him, each person could be using the word "beetle" to refer to a different object, or indeed nothing at all. Similarly, if sensations were intrinsically private, no word (or indeed any other type of sign) could be used intelligibly to refer to a sensation because there would be no visible, public criterion of correctness for the use of the word.

Second, if learning the correct concept to refer to a sensation consisted of associating the concept with a sensation that only the language learner could feel and know to be present, then the concept could not even be used intelligibly by the language learner herself. The language learner who learns the concept "pain" to refer to the sensation of pain needs a criterion of correctness, something by which to judge whether she is using the concept to refer to the sensation of pain, instead of some other sensation. But what could function as a criterion of correctness if sensations were intrinsically private? The language learner might respond that, whenever she feels what she thinks is the sensation of pain, she appeals to her memory to see if it is indeed the sensation of pain, and if it is, she uses the concept "pain" to refer to it. However, this is unintelligible.

To verify whether she is correct in calling a certain sensation "pain," the language learner is appealing to her memory of pain. But it is precisely her memory of pain that she is attempting to verify (PI §265). Such a process of verification is as illogical as buying several copies of the morning paper to assure oneself that what is said there is true (PI §265). At the very most, such a language learner would be able to make "sounds which no one else understands" while pretending to understand them (PI §269).

The concepts that we use to refer to inner mental life, just like any concepts, require public, visible criteria of correctness in order to be used intelligibly. In other words, a language user must be able to appeal to criteria of correctness when using concepts of the inner, or when judging if they are being used correctly by others. If he could not appeal to them because they were private and invisible, the language learner would not know how to use concepts of the inner correctly, or be able to challenge their incorrect use on the part of another, as we have just seen in the examples provided by Wittgenstein. Anthony Kenny clarifies what Wittgenstein means by a criterion for a mental state by contrasting it with a symptom, another type of evidence. A symptom of a state of affairs is discovered through empirical inquiry. For example, certain electrical brain patterns may be discovered to be associated with the capacity to speak the English language by experiments showing that the brains of English speakers exhibit such patterns while the brains of non-English speakers don't. A criterion, in contrast, is not discovered by empirical inquiry but is something that must be known in advance by anyone who possesses the concept in question. A person's capacity to speak English, for example, is not just a symptom of, but a criterion for, his possession of English. In other words, mastery of the concept "possession of English" involves learning that the capacity to speak English indicates its possession. This is not discovered through empirical inquiry but is learned when the concept of possessing English is learned.[42]

What, therefore, do function as the public, visible criteria of correctness for the use of concepts of the inner? Wittgenstein answers by examining how human beings actually learn words for sensations and other inner phenomena—what infants are taught regarding the actual criteria for concepts of the inner. Infants, he argues, are taught to replace pain-behavior by the word "pain," thereby learning that, for us, pain behavior constitutes the criterion for the presence of pain in human beings and other creatures like them (PI §244). Pain behavior is not something superfluous to what we call pain, as if pain was intrinsically private and could exist independently of pain behavior. Rather pain and pain behavior are logically connected. The latter constitutes the public, visible criterion for the presence of the former.

The conclusion drawn by most of Wittgenstein's interpreters from these private language arguments is that the notion of an intrinsically private mental object, state, event, or process—one that has no necessary or logical connection to outer behavior—is nonsensical.[43] Instead, these arguments show that it is outer behavior—typical bodily and linguistic manifestations and expressions, patterns of antecedent and consequent behavior—within an enormous variety of finely differentiated contexts that constitute the criteria for the application of concepts of the inner. These outer behavioral criteria are logically connected to our concepts of the inner and hence cannot discarded. Attempts to define and use concepts of the inner independently of such outer behavioral criteria fail.

Hence, Balázs's claim that mental life—or at least a certain dimension of mental life—cannot be expressed in modernity is nonsensical. According to Wittgenstein, the inner is logically dependent on outer behavior. We say that we see that another human being is in pain (e.g., a man screaming in agony after being knocked down by a car) because behavior such as screaming in the context of being knocked down by a car constitutes one of the criteria for being in pain. This man's pain behavior is not a superfluous, dispensable addition to our seeing that he is in pain. Rather, screaming in agony in the context of being knocked down by a car is what we call being in pain. To see him behaving in this way in this context is to see that he is in pain. If human beings suddenly stopped expressing their emotions and other mental phenomena, as Balázs argues has occurred in modernity, these emotions would not exist "unexpressed," as he claims. Rather, our concepts of the inner would become unusable and meaningless, and we would no longer be able to conceive of emotions, unexpressed or not. Like the beetle in the box, they would drop "out of consideration as irrelevant" (PI §293). Moreover, as anyone who has witnessed a car accident knows, people continue to scream in agony, cry out of sadness, and in various other ways manifest their emotions physically in modernity. The body has not forgotten how to express them, and nor has the eye forgotten how to see them. Thus, we do not need the cinema to reveal them in the way that we need a telescope to reveal a distant planet. Unless our sense of sight is impaired, we can see them perfectly well unaided.

Kracauer's theory focuses on quotidian phenomena typically encountered in everyday life by humans in modern societies. According to Kracauer, even though people regularly encounter quotidian phenomena, these phenomena are invisible to them until the cinema reveals them. As he puts it:

> In recording and exploring physical reality, film exposes to view a world never seen before, a world as elusive as Poe's purloined letter, which cannot be found because it is within everybody's reach. What is meant here is of course not any of those extensions of the everyday world which are being annexed by science but our ordinary physical environment itself. Strange as it may seem, although streets, faces, railway stations, etc., lie before our eyes, they have remained largely invisible so far.[44]

Kracauer's theory of what the cinema reveals, however, turns out to be another example of what Ryle calls a category mistake. Kracauer confuses one type of phenomenon—things that we sometimes do not pay attention to, or notice, or see fully, or that we cannot see at certain moments in time due to viewing circumstances, or because they are hidden from us—with another—phenomena that are invisible in the sense that we cannot see them unaided and that need to be revealed by a visual technology in order to be seen.

According to Kracauer, as we saw in chapter 1, our ordinary physical environment is largely invisible to us because we cannot see the qualities of things as a result of the abstractness of modernity. "Quality" is a vague concept, and Kracauer does not explicitly clarify the sense in which he is using the word in his theory. Indeed, for somebody who criticizes abstractions, Kracauer's theory is remarkably abstract—he gives very few concrete examples of qualities that he believes sight is incapable of seeing unaided. One example he does give is Alfred Whitehead's example of the radiance of a sunset, which Kracauer quotes verbatim: "When you understand all about the sun and all about the atmosphere and all about the rotation of the earth, you may still miss the radiance of the sunset" (TF 296). And what this example, and his argument (which we have already surveyed) about abstractness in modernity seem to suggest is that, for Kracauer, a quality is a unique, physical characteristic of an object or event, something specific or particular to it, that cannot be captured by abstract categories. When we look at a sunset in modernity, according to this argument, what we see is a generic sunset because we subsume it under abstract categories applicable to sunsets in general—in all sunsets, the sun appears to move downward behind the horizon, the light fades, and so on. What we do not see are this particular sunset's unique physical characteristics, such as the specific color and intensity of its radiance.

This argument will doubtless be familiar to anybody who is acquainted with neo-Kantian aesthetic theories, and it is therefore susceptible to all of the standard criticisms leveled at such theories. For example, critics often point out that, far from preventing us from seeing the unique physical characteristics of an object or event, so-called abstract categories enable us to see them. For it is only if we are aware of the degree of radiance of a particular sunset relative to sunsets in general that we can see its particular radiance. The particular only stands out against the general. But the point that is relevant to my argument in this book is that, in claiming that we do not attend to qualities in modernity and that they are therefore invisible to us and need to be revealed by a visual technology in order to be seen, Kracauer makes the category mistake described above. For we do not say that something is invisible if we do not pay attention to it. Indeed, in order to be able to attend, or fail to attend, to something, it must be visible. Right now, sitting at my desk in my office writing these sentences on my computer, I am not paying attention to what is outside of the window behind me. But this does not mean that what is outside of the window is invisible and needs to be revealed by a visual technology in order to be seen—it simply means that I am not attending to it. And in order for me to be able to attend to it by walking over to the window and looking out, what is outside of the window must be visible. With phenomena that we do speak of as being invisible in the sense that we cannot see them unaided, such as microbes and ultraviolet light, we cannot see them simply by attending to them because something about their very nature (size in the case of microbes and frequency in the case of ultraviolet light) makes it impossible for us to see them unaided. Nor is it because of some way in which modernity has altered my mind that I cannot see them unaided. Even if I lived in premodern times, I would not be able to see microbes or ultraviolet light without a visual technology.

Furthermore, we do not speak of something that makes us attend to something we are not paying attention to as revealing it. If somebody comes in to my office and tells me to look out of the window behind me, we do not say that this person is revealing what is outside of the window to me. Rather, we say that he or she is directing my attention to something that I was not paying attention to before. Meanwhile, a microscope reveals a microbe to me not by making me pay attention to it, but by magnifying it so that I can see it. Kracauer confuses the category of phenomena we do not pay attention to with the category of phenomena that we cannot see unaided because something about their nature makes them invisible to the human eye, a confusion that is often evident in his writing: "Film renders visible what we *did not,* or perhaps even *could not,* see before its advent" (TF 300; my emphasis). If Kracauer is correct and it is only when watching films that we see the qualities of objects, this is not because these qualities are invisible and are revealed to us by the cinema. Rather, it is because we attend to qualities only when watching films.

Kracauer makes the same category mistake with many of the other phenomena that he argues are revealed by the cinema. He begins his list of "things normally unseen" by sight with "objects too small to be readily noticed or even perceived by the naked eye," and gives as an example a close-up of "Mae Marsh's clasped hands in the trial episode of *Intolerance*" (TF 46–47). According to Kracauer, this close-up "reveals how her hands behave under the impact of utter despair" (TF 47). But we would not say that this close-up is revealing something that can only be seen with a visual technology. Rather, we would say that it is revealing something that, due to viewing circumstances, we had not noticed or been able to see prior to the close-up. At this moment, I cannot see the title on the spine of a book that is in a bookcase in my office because of a viewing circumstance—the desk I am sitting at is too far away from it. But while we might say that the title is invisible to me at this moment because it is too far away, we would not say that it is invisible to me in the sense that I need a visual technology to reveal it. For if I moved close enough to it, I would be able to see it unaided. Similarly, the viewer cannot see Mae Marsh's hands and the emotions they express due to viewing circumstances, the way the scene has been filmed prior to the close-up (the camera is too far away from her, her hands are concealed by the mise-en-scene, etc.). The shot that does reveal her hands changes the viewing circumstances because it is filmed close enough to her hands that the viewer can see them. Phenomena that we describe as invisible in the sense of being impossible to see unaided cannot be seen by the naked human eye no matter what the viewing circumstances and hence must be revealed by a visual technology in order to be seen. I cannot see ultraviolet light just by moving closer to it or by filming it in close-up.

There is another sense in which Mae Marsh's hands can be said to be invisible until they are revealed by Griffith's close-up: they are hidden from the viewer. We often speak of something being invisible if it is hidden. But to be invisible in the sense of being hidden is not to be invisible in the sense of being impossible to see unaided. I have a bad photograph of myself hidden in my desk in my office, so that colleagues and students cannot see it. It therefore can be said to be invisible to them. However, I have hidden it precisely because it would be visible to them if I had not. But whether I hid a microbe or not, it would still be invisible to me because it is too small for me to see it unaided. In the case of "the small," Kracauer is confusing phenomena that, due to viewing circumstances or being hidden, we cannot see at certain moments in time, with phenomena such as microbes that are impossible for us to see unaided no matter the viewing circumstances or whether they are hidden and that therefore need to be revealed by a visual technology in order to be seen.

Following "the small," Kracauer suggests that "objects so big" that they "elude observation" are also an example of one of the cinema's "revealing functions" (TF 46), and he claims that "among the large objects, such as vast plains or panoramas of any kind, one deserves special attention: the masses" (TF 50). Only photography and film, he argues, can "portray crowds as the accidental conglomerations they are," and he says that "the traditional arts" are "unable to encompass and render" crowds—only film can do this while also "capturing them in motion" (TF 50). But as these quotations suggest in their use of verbs such as "portraying," "capturing," and "rendering" instead of "revealing," we do not speak of crowds and other large phenomena as being invisible and therefore in need of being revealed by a visual technology in order to be seen just because we are unable to see them in their entirety. If I stand in the middle of a desert, I am unable to see the entire desert. But this does not mean that the desert is invisible to me, for desert surrounds me as far as the eye can see. Nor would we say that a visual technology that shows the desert in its entirety—an aerial photograph, for example—reveals the desert. Rather, we would say that it reveals the desert in its entirety. Here, it is phenomena that are too big to be seen in their entirety that Kracauer has conflated with phenomena that are invisible and need to be revealed by a visual technology in order to be seen.

After "the big," Kracauer argues that another "group of things normally unseen comprises the transient," and he gives as examples phenomena that are "imperceptible" to the naked human eye because they happen too slowly, such as the growth of plants, as well as things "too fast to be registered" by the eye such as the "racing legs" of galloping horses. While one might question whether such phenomena are best described as "transient," it makes sense to call them invisible and in need of revelation by a visual technology in order to be seen. For these are phenomena that, due to something about their nature (the speed at which they occur, in this case) cannot be seen by the naked human eye, rather than things that are visible but that we sometimes do not pay attention to, or notice, or see fully, or that we cannot see at certain moments in time due to viewing circumstances, or because they are hidden from us. And, because of the techniques of fast and slow motion, the cinema is indeed able to reveal them. Kracauer is here appealing to the perfectly acceptable use of the cinema to reveal phenomena, such as the leg positions of galloping horses or the wing movements of birds, that I mentioned in the introduction. But he also cites under the category of the transient phenomena the mane of a galloping horse,

as well as "the shadow of a cloud passing across the plain," without providing any explanation as to why they are invisible to human vision and need to
be revealed by a visual technology in order to be seen. These phenomena are
neither too fast nor too slow to be perceived by the naked eye; we can, and
regularly do, see them perfectly well unaided. Here, Kracauer seems to be
conflating phenomena that move ("the transient") with phenomena that move
too quickly or too slowly to be seen by the naked human eye.

The final category of phenomena that Kracauer argues is revealed by the
cinema is what he calls "blind spots of the mind," and he includes under it
"refuse" such as "garbage," as well as things that are familiar to us, such as
"streets we walk day by day" (TF 54–55). But again, just because we do not
usually pay attention to garbage, or the streets we often walk down, does not
mean that they are invisible to us and in need of being revealed by a visual
technology in order to be seen, for reasons I surveyed when I examined qualities. These things must be visible to the naked human eye in order for us to fail
to attend to them. Meanwhile, it is not because I fail to attend to ultraviolet
light that I cannot see it, for no amount of attending to it will enable me to see
it without a visual technology.

Another example Kracauer gives of blind spots of the mind is what he
refers to as "unconventional complexes," which he defines as "previously invisible interrelationships between parts" of objects (TF 54). By this, he seems
to mean abstract patterns formed by concrete objects or their parts. As he puts
it, "in rendering physical existence, film tends to reveal configurations of semiabstract phenomena," and he gives as an example a scene from *Triumph of
the Will* in which "moving banners fuse into a very beautiful pattern at the
moment when they begin to fill the screen" (TF 54). Here, Kracauer is characterizing something that we do not always notice as something that we cannot
see because it is invisible. As I look at the peeling paint of my office wall,
I notice an abstract pattern among the paint chips akin to a magnified snowflake.
I have never noticed it before, even though I have contemplated the peeling
paint many times. We would not say, however, that this pattern was invisible to
me before I noticed it, because, as with paying attention, something has to be
visible in order to fail to notice it. There is nothing about the nature of abstract
patterns that makes them impossible to see unaided. While it may be true that
the cinema can draw our attention to abstract patterns in reality through editing, framing, and other techniques, this does not mean it is revealing something
that was previously invisible. Furthermore, it is usually the case that films *create* abstract patterns that do not exist in reality, rather than revealing ones that
do exist. For example, in *October*, Eisenstein creates graphic discontinuity between shots of flags by juxtaposing a shot of a flag that flows diagonally from
the top left to the bottom right of the screen with a shot of a flag that flows
from the top right to the bottom left. This is an abstract pattern created out of
camera position, framing, editing, and the plastic properties of flags. It is not a
preexisting abstract pattern that Eisenstein is revealing.

The final two categories of phenomena that Kracauer lists under the
cinema's revealing functions are what he calls "phenomena overwhelming

consciousness" and "special modes of reality." The former he defines in the following way:

> Elemental catastrophes, the atrocities of war, acts of violence and terror, sexual debauchery, and death are events which tend to overwhelm consciousness. In any case, they call forth excitements and agonies bound to thwart detached observation. No one witnessing such an event, let alone playing an active part in it, should therefore be expected accurately to account for what he has seen. . . . Only the camera is able to represent them without distortion. (TF 57)

What Kracauer seems to be arguing here is that, due to their extreme nature, certain acts and events are so emotionally and intellectually overwhelming that viewers cannot remember and represent them accurately. Meanwhile, because it is a machine, the cinema records them "without distortion." As for special modes of reality, Kracauer gives as an example the scene from *October* in which some Cossacks defect to the Bolshevik side and celebrate by dancing. Eisenstein's use of fast, discontinuous editing and close-ups to film the dance represent, according to Kracauer, the way it appears to the soldiers in their state of happiness. "In their great joy, dancers and onlookers who constantly mingle cannot help perceiving incoherent pieces of their immediate environment in motion. It is a whirling agglomerate of fragments that surrounds them. And Eisenstein captures this jumble to perfection" (TF 59). For Kracauer, this is an example of how the cinema can "expose physical reality as it appears to individuals in extreme states of mind" (TF 58). Kracauer here seems to be referring to what today we would call subjective narration, the representation of aspects of subjective experience, such as the appearance something has for a person in a certain state of mind, with stylistic techniques such as point-of-view shots, editing, anamorphic lenses, camera movement, and the like. A standard example is the use of free-wheeling camera movement to represent the way the world appears to rock from side to side to a drunken person, as when the major protagonist is drunk in *The Last Laugh* (1924).

Kracauer does not, however, argue that phenomena overwhelming consciousness and special modes of reality are invisible and need to be revealed by a visual technology in order to be seen, instead separating them from what he calls "things normally unseen" (TF 46). In these instances, he does not transgress the bounds of sense, although he does come perilously close on occasion, claiming, for example, that the cinema "insists on rendering visible what is commonly drowned in inner agitation" (TF 58), as if to suggest that phenomena overwhelming consciousness are invisible. But in order to fail to remember and represent such phenomena accurately, as Kracauer himself acknowledges elsewhere, observers have first to see ("witness") them (TF 57). Such acts and events are not invisible and in need of being revealed by a visual technology. Rather, once seen, they are difficult to remember accurately and in need of being recorded.

In the case of special modes of reality, while we might say that, in a scene such as the one from *October,* the cinema is revealing the way something appears to someone, we would not say that it is revealing it in the sense of bringing to view something otherwise invisible. When a visual technology reveals something invisible, it does so by showing it in such a way that a viewer can see it or its previously invisible properties. When the cinema reveals the precise wing movement of a bird, it does so by recording the bird in flight and then showing it in slow motion so that the viewer can see its previously invisible wing movement. But in the scene from *October,* the cinema is not recording the dance and then showing it in such a way that the viewer can see something about the dance that was previously invisible. For the appearance of something to somebody is not a property of that thing, in the way that wing movement is a property of a bird. The world does not really rock from side to side when a person is drunk. A dance is not really a "whirling agglomerate of fragments." Rather, in these cases, certain stylistic techniques are being used to *create* a rough approximation for the viewer of the appearance of the world when drunk and of the dance to the soldiers when happy. These techniques are not bringing to view a property of the world or the dance that would otherwise be invisible. In this way, these techniques are like the discontinuous shifts in scale and point-of-view used by painters such as Fernand Léger to represent the appearance of the modern environment in their paintings. A city is not really a "rush of images assaulting the eye simultaneously," which is how Standish Lawder describes the appearance of the city in Léger's painting *La Ville* (1919).[45] This is not an otherwise invisible property of the city that Leger is revealing in his painting. Rather, Léger is using discontinuous shifts in scale and point-of-view to create for the viewer a rough approximation of the way the city appears to an observer.

Why do we say that the cinema is revealing the way the dance appears to the happy soldiers in the scene from *October* if it is not bringing to view an otherwise invisible property of the dance? We do so, of course, because to reveal means not only to bring to view but to make known. We use the word to reveal not only in the context of vision but in the context of knowledge. Seeing need not be involved in revealing. A friend can, for example, reveal a secret verbally over the phone. In the case of the scene from *October,* we say that Eisenstein's techniques are revealing the way the dance appears to the happy soldiers because we would not have *known* it otherwise, not because we would not have *seen* it otherwise.

While Kracauer does, for the most part, use the concepts of invisibility and revelation correctly when discussing phenomena overwhelming consciousness and special modes of reality, as we have seen, elsewhere he systematically conflates things that are visible but that we sometimes do not pay attention to, or notice, or see fully, or that we cannot see at certain moments in time due to viewing circumstances, or because they are hidden from us, with things that are invisible in the sense that the eye is too weak to see them and that therefore need to be revealed by a visual technology in order to be seen. Like Balázs and Epstein (in certain instances), he denies sight the capacity to see phenomena—the particular radiance of a particular sunset, hands, deserts, the mane of a galloping horse, refuse, and so on—that can be seen perfectly well unaided, and he does so through a systematic misuse of perceptual concepts such as invisibility.

3

Revelationism and Contemporary Film Theory

Not long after the publication of Kracauer's *Theory of Film* in 1960, a new type of film theory emerged that was dominated by two theoretical paradigms: semiotics and psychoanalysis. Due to the influence of the New Left as well as various political and social upheavals during the 1960s, the new semiotic-psychoanalytical film theory was preoccupied with a question about the cinema that, while asked to some extent by earlier film theorists, was less important to them than questions about the cinema's nature and artistic value: how does the cinema propagate ideology? Before the 1960s, film theorists for the most part viewed the cinema as morally and politically benign, at least when it was being used to create art.[1] Some, as I have already described, went further and argued that the cinema could be used to transform society for the better. Semiotic-psychoanalytical film theorists, in contrast, saw the cinema as politically and morally pernicious. And this was because, unlike earlier film theorists who, if they did examine ideology, focused for the most part on specific films,[2] the new theorists argued that ideology is reproduced by the basic properties or features of the cinema—the technologies used to produce and exhibit films (the camera, its lens, the projector) as well as its predominant forms (narrative, documentary) and stylistic norms (continuity editing).[3]

At first glance, therefore, it may seem that the revelationist tradition fell into obsolescence in the 1960s. Semiotic-psychoanalytical film theorists viewed the cinema as a tool of deception rather than enlightenment. They saw cinema as something that, far from revealing truths about reality, propagates false beliefs about it. And in place of the revelationist tradition's enchantment concerning the cinema's revelatory power, we find in the new theory disenchantment due to the belief that the cinema deceives people and thereby transforms society for the worse. But in fact, despite appearances to the contrary, semiotic-psychoanalytical film theory was greatly indebted to the revelationist tradition. Whether knowingly or not, it borrowed and renewed this tradition's fundamental tenets.[4]

First, the new theory evinced a pervasive distrust of human vision. For the new theorists, just as much as for their predecessors, sight was fundamentally flawed. However, they renewed this visual skepticism by turning to powerful new theories to justify it, those of Marx and Freud as filtered through the writings of Louis Althusser and Jacques Lacan as well as Bertolt Brecht's writings on the theater. And they mobilized a concept that, while present to some extent in previous film theorizing, became central to film theory after 1968: the concept of illusion.

According to Althusser and Lacan, humans have a mistaken view of themselves. In capitalist societies, Althusser argued, people believe that they are autonomous agents with free will (subjects), when in fact they are controlled by (subject to) the capitalist social formation. According to Althusser, this false belief is perpetuated by "ideological state apparatuses," various institutions, such as the government, the church, and the media, that address humans as if they were subjects (interpellation).[5] And the reason people mistake being addressed as subjects for being subjects is because they misrecognize themselves, Lacan argued. For Lacan, humans are born into a condition of "no-thing-ness," of psychic fragmentation and dispersal in which there is no distinction between self and other.[6] As a child develops, he forms an image of himself (the ego) as an autonomous, unified entity separate from the world around him. However, this image is an illusion because the real condition of the subject, Lacan believed, remains no-thing-ness ("the Real").[7] Althusser used a version of this argument to explain why people falsely believe that they are what the ideological state apparatuses tell them that they are: autonomous, free agents or subjects. It is because people falsely believe that they are subjects and have freely chosen the social roles that capitalism has imposed on them, he claimed, that the capitalist social formation can reproduce itself even though it is exploitative.[8]

Semiotic-psychoanalytical film theorists, following Althusser and Lacan, conceived of humans as laboring under an epistemic illusion, the false belief that they are subjects. But Lacan also provided film theorists with the conceptual tool to renew skepticism about vision by arguing that this epistemic illusion is reproduced, in part, in the realm of sight. Between the ages of six and eighteen months, Lacan argued, infants begin to look at and recognize themselves in mirrors. However, they mistake the image of themselves that they see in the mirror, in which they appear autonomous and unified, for truth. They identify (primary identification) with this image in the sense of taking it as an accurate representation of themselves (the ego), even though they remain in the condition of no-thing-ness. Lacan used the mirror stage as an allegory for the formation of human subjectivity and believed that, as they learn language and enter society ("the Symbolic"), people constantly search out representations of themselves which, like the mirror image of the mirror stage, they mistake for truth and with which they identify ("the Imaginary").[9]

Although Lacan was not only referring to sight in his arguments about the Imaginary, the fact that he claimed that humans do, at least in the mirror stage, literally mistake images of themselves for truth gave semiotic-psychoanalytical film theorists the theoretical ammunition to renew skepticism about human vision. For them, sight was to be distrusted, at least in part, because it helps reproduce the epistemic illusion that humans are subjects by mistaking false images of the self as unified and autonomous for reality. However, it was the confluence of this argument about vision with Bertolt Brecht's (also in vogue in the 1960s and employed by Althusser as well as influential filmmakers such as Jean-Luc Godard) that truly enabled the new generation of film theorists to renew skepticism about sight. Brecht's writings contain a variety of sometimes inconsistent claims. Nevertheless, like Althusser and Lacan, at least sometimes he argued that humans mistake representations for truth, and, like Althusser, that this mistake serves the economic interests of the ruling class. And he claimed (again sometimes) that this mistake occurs in the realm of fiction, specifically theatrical fiction, in the form of an epistemic and visual illusion of the following kind:

> Above all, the Chinese artist never acts as if there were a fourth wall besides the three surrounding him. He expresses his awareness of being watched. This immediately removes one of the European stage's characteristic illusions. The audience can no longer have the illusion of being the unseen spectator at an event which is really taking place.[10]

In conjunction with the Lacanian claim that the epistemic illusion of being a unified, autonomous subject is reproduced in the realm of sight, this argument about the propensity of spectators to experience the epistemic and visual illusion of being an "unseen spectator at an event which is really taking place," when extended to the cinema, proved to be a potent enough form of skepticism about vision to dominate Anglo-American film theorizing until well into the 1980s. For semiotic-psychoanalytical film theorists, the eye could not be trusted because it mistakes representations—cinematic representations, and representations of the self—for reality.

Unlike theorists in the revelationist tradition, the new theorists did not view the cinema's properties as enabling an escape from the limitations of sight, from the epistemic and visual illusions it is prone to. As we have seen, Epstein, Vertov, Balázs, and Kracauer argued that the cinema's features—editing (Vertov), the close-up (Epstein and Balázs), and recording (Kracauer), among others—could be exploited to escape the flaws of human vision. The new theory, however, turned this argument on its head by claiming that the cinema's properties reinforce these flaws, vision's propensity to experience epistemic and visual illusions.

For example, in *The Imaginary Signifier*, one of the most influential and famous works of semiotic-psychoanalytical film theory, Christian Metz argued that "film is like the mirror" of the mirror stage because, like a mirror, what it represents is absent (from the representation), while the representation itself is present.[11] Because the play of presence and absence in the cinematic image is like the play of presence and absence in the mirror, it facilitates the same process of "primary identification (the formation of the ego)" that takes place in the mirror stage. However, due to the fact that the cinematic image is not literally a mirror—the viewer cannot literally see a reflection of himself in it—the viewer does not identify with his own image, as does the child in the mirror stage. Instead, he identifies with the perceptual experience he has while in the cinema ("the spectator *identifies with himself,* with himself as a pure act of perception") and therefore with what creates this experience ("as he identifies with himself as look, the spectator can do no other than identify with the camera, too").[12] He takes what the camera has recorded as his own percepts, thereby experiencing the epistemic and visual illusion that he is seeing reality rather than a filmic representation. For the camera is "all perceiving":

> All-perceiving as one says all-powerful (this is the famous gift of "ubiquity" the film makes its spectator); all-perceiving, too, because I am entirely on the side of the perceiving instance: absent from the screen, but certainly present in the auditorium, a great eye and ear without which the perceived would have no one to perceive it, the instance, in other words, which *constitutes* the cinema signifier (it is I who make the film).[13]

Just as the infant identifies with its mirror image in the mirror stage, mistaking the image of herself as autonomous and unified for truth, so the viewer identifies with the perceptual experience created for her by the cinema, mistaking the experience of autonomy and unity it affords her ("all-perceiving") for her own ("it is I who make the film"). Although semiotic-psychoanalytical film theorists disagreed about precisely how the cinema does this, they all tended to argue, like Metz, that it gives rise to two types of epistemic and visual illusion: the illusion that one is a unified, autonomous subject, and the illusion that one is in the presence of reality rather than a representation.

The second way in which semiotic-psychoanalytical film theory was indebted to the revelationist tradition is perhaps less obvious. It may appear, from what I have said so far, that the new theorists no longer viewed the cinema as an artistic medium that reveals truths about reality. For as we have just seen, they conceived of the cinema's basic features as propagating false beliefs about reality in the form of epistemic and visual illusions. Yet, in fact, the new theory advocated a type of film art that compensates for the propensity of sight to experience illusions by revealing the truths about reality that these illusions mask. And in advocating this type of film art, the new theory, once again, renewed its revelationist predecessor, this time in much the same way that Symbolism renewed Romanticism a century earlier. Charles Taylor has described this renewal in the following way:

> An influential strand of thought from the Symbolists on has conceived of the work not as an epiphany of being, either of nature or of a spiritual reality beyond nature [as the Romantics did]. They have tried to detach it from all relation to what is beyond it and yet, paradoxically, to retain the epiphanic quality. The work remains the locus of revelation, and of something of ultimate significance, but it is also utterly self-contained and self-sufficient.[14]

It is this type of art, the "autotelic," in which the locus of revelation shifts to within the work of art itself, that semiotic-psychoanalytical film theory championed. Whereas the revelationist tradition conceived of the cinema as revealing truths about reality by making visible something external to the cinema—emotion (Epstein), class relations (Vertov), the inner (Balázs), and qualities (Kracauer), among others—the new theorists conceived of the cinema as revealing truths about reality by making visible its own internal properties and conventions, a process that came to be known as "reflexivity."

Semiotic-psychoanalytical film theorists advocated a variety of different types of reflexive film art, even finding reflexivity in Hollywood films such as the 1950s melodramas of Douglas Sirk. However, perhaps the most pure, extreme example was the structural-materialist avant-garde film lauded by the British journal *Screen* in the 1970s.[15] Structural-materialist filmmakers did not rest content with simply revealing the cinema's properties and the various conventions that govern its most common forms (narrative, documentary); they also argued that a reflexive film art should reveal to the viewer the process through which these properties and conventions form the finished film and the viewer's experience of it. As Stephen Heath put it,

> Materialist stresses process, a film in its process of production of images, sounds, times, meanings, the transformations effected on the basis of the specific properties of film in the relation of a viewing and listening situation. It is that situation which is, finally, the point of "structural/materialist film," its fundamental operation, the *experience* of film and the experience *of film.*[16]

Hence, in many structuralist-materialist films, rather than a representation of something we get a coming-into-being of a representation of something, a representation in the process of being formed, such as in Peter Gidal's *Room Film* (1973), in which hand-held panning shots of a room constantly go in and out of focus. In its emphasis on process, structural-materialist film probably came closer than any other type of reflexive cinema to what Taylor, as noted above, described as a work that remains the locus of revelation but that is also self-contained and self-sufficient. Although not many new theorists went as far as advocating such an extreme, iconoclastic (and iconophobic) avant-garde artistic practice, they all tended to promote an autotelic or reflexive cinema.

But what truths about reality does reflexivity reveal, according to semiotic-psychoanalytical film theorists? How does reflexivity compensate for the susceptibility of human vision to visual and epistemic illusions? First, and most obviously, it does so by breaking the illusion postulated by ciné-Brechtians, the illusion that the viewer is in the presence of reality when watching a film. In doing so, it reveals the truth masked by this illusion—namely, the film itself. By drawing the viewer's attention to the properties, conventions, and processes of the cinema, reflexivity forces the viewer to see what he is really in the presence of: a film, not reality. Second, according to the new theorists, reflexivity shatters the illusion theorized by Althusser and Lacan: the viewer's mistaken belief that he is a subject, an autonomous, free, unified agent. The truth masked by this illusion is thereby revealed to the viewer: his no-thing-ness. Heath made this argument in relation to structural-materialist film by claiming that, because the various cinematic properties and processes revealed by structuralist-materialist films are heterogeneous in nature, the viewer who watches a structuralist-materialist film is plunged into a state of psychic heterogeneity.

> The contrary practice of "structural-materialist film" is to break given terms of unity, to explore the heterogeneity of film in process. . . . The disunity, the disjunction, of "structural-materialist film" is, exactly, the spectator. What is intended, what the practice addresses, is not a spectator as unified subject . . . but a spectator, a spectating activity, at the limit of any fixed subjectivity, materially inconstant, dispersed in process, beyond the accommodation of reality and pleasure principles.[17]

While Heath's arguments here are specific to structuralist-materialist film, semiotic-psychoanalytical film theorists all tended to argue that reflexivity breaks the viewer's illusion that he is an autonomous, unified subject.

Given its renewal of skepticism about human vision, it should come as no surprise that the new theory was continuous with its revelationist predecessor in yet another way. We saw in chapter 2 how theorists in the revelationist tradition arrived at their distrust of sight primarily by confusing things that it is logically impossible for human beings to see with empirical phenomena the naked eye is too weak to see and by denying sight the capacity to see things that it can see perfectly well unaided. Semiotic-psychoanalytical film theorists were no different in their misuse (indeed abuse) of the concept of illusion.

A visual illusion is something that, by way of its appearance, deceives the person experiencing it into believing or perceiving something that is not true. As we have seen, the new theorists argued that when watching a film, viewers experience the epistemic and visual illusion that they are in the presence of reality rather than a representation. However, as Noël Carroll and others have argued, this claim is demonstrably false. First of all, viewers of films do not normally behave as they would if this claim were true. For example, they do not typically flee movie theaters seeking to protect themselves as, presumably, they would if they believed that they were in the presence of reality when watching horror films, disaster films, science-fiction films, and action films. Second, and relatedly, mistaking a fiction for reality would in many cases prevent viewers from appreciating the fiction, thereby undermining the whole point of fiction. As Carroll puts it in relation to horror fictions:

> If when reading or viewing fictions we come to be convinced, albeit by deception, that werewolves really existed in our vicinity, it would be difficult to continue to savor the story. One would want to take some practical measures to secure one's life and loved ones. A very condition of there being an institution of fiction from which we derive entertainment and pleasure is that we know that the persons and events are not actual.[18]

Third, unlike trompe-oeils and other visual illusions, films are not standardly designed to deceive their viewers that they are in the presence of reality rather than a representation. They lack three-dimensionality; frequently move through space and time via editing and camera movement; are often accompanied by extra-diegetic music and subtitles; regularly employ patently unrealistic staging, lighting, setting, costume, make-up, and color; and use out-of-focus, high, low, and tilted camera angles, and so on. Although it might be possible to design and exhibit a film in such a way that it deceives its viewers into believing that they are in the presence of reality, films are not typically designed this way.

These are just some of the arguments that have been leveled against semiotic-psychoanalytical film theory's claim that the cinema deceives viewers epistemically and visually into mistaking a representation for reality.[19] The point of mentioning them here is to show that, like their predecessors in the revelationist tradition, the new theorists arrived at their distrust of vision through a misuse of perceptual concepts, in this case the concept of a visual illusion. They denied sight the capacity to see something that it can see perfectly well unaided: that a film is a representation, not reality.

Richard Allen has attempted to rehabilitate the concept of illusion for film theory by distinguishing between illusions that give rise to false beliefs and illusions that deceive the senses but do not result in false beliefs. A trompe-l'oeil is a canonical example of the former because it can deceive the viewer into believing that what it depicts is real. The famous Müller-Lyer illusion is an example of the latter, because lines of equal length are perceived as unequal even when the viewer knows that they are equal and has no false belief about their length. Allen suggests that when we view film and other visual representations, we can have an illusion of the latter type, one in which no false belief is involved. We can experience the representation as "a fully realized world of experience and not a representation," even though we know it is a representation.[20] He calls this projective illusion, and argues that it happens as a result of imagining that we see what the representation depicts. However, we do not have to experience a visual representation this way, he claims. This is because, unlike the case of the Müller-Lyer illusion, "our knowledge about what we are seeing can break the hold of the illusion."[21] Allen argues that when viewing a visual representation we can flip-flop between being aware of it as a representation and the experience of projective illusion, just as when looking at Jastrow's duck-rabbit figure we can flip-flop between seeing the figure as a duck and seeing it as a rabbit.

> When you see a zombie in George Romero's *Night of the Living Dead* (1968), you may see the image as a medium-aware spectator. That is, you may look through the image at the fictional portrayal of a zombie not only with the knowledge that what you see is only a film, but also by perceiving the way in which the fictional scene is staged for the camera. . . . However, there is [another] option: You may imagine that you perceive a world inhabited by zombies. In this . . . case, you do not mistake a staged event for actuality; . . . rather, you lose awareness of the fact that you are seeing a film, that is, watching a recorded event that is staged before the camera. . . . You perceive a fully realized though fictional world that has all the perceptual immediacy of our own; you experience the film as a projective illusion.[22]

This is an intriguing argument, but once again it only gets off the ground because of a misuse of the concept of illusion. An illusion is not something that we can *choose* to experience. Rather, an illusion is something that happens to the senses, which is why we speak of illusions as deceiving us. I can perhaps choose to experience an illusion in the sense of creating a situation in which I am likely to experience one, for example by arranging objects in my environment in such a way that they appear to be closer or bigger than they really are. But I cannot do so in the sense of simply willing it to happen or imagining that it does. When looking at the Müller-Lyer illusion, for example, I cannot flip-flop back and forth at will between experiencing it as an illusion in which I see the lines as unequal in length and experiencing it as a representation in which I see the true length of the lines. Rather, I both experience it as a representation and as an illusion the entire time. Allen acknowledges that projective illusion is un-like the Müller-Lyer illusion in this respect. Instead, he claims, it is more like a mirror illusion in which we initially mistake a mirror image of something for the thing itself. When we find out that we are seeing a mirror image, this knowledge breaks the hold of the illusion, he argues. But this analogy does not help Allen's argument, because once again we cannot choose to see a mirror image as an illusion. If the illusion is effective, it appears as if we are seeing the thing the mirror reflects rather than a mirror image of it, regardless of whether we know it is an illusion. We cannot, in other words, flip-flop back and forth at will between seeing the mirror image as an illusion and seeing it as a mirror image as we can, according to Allen, in the case of projective illusion. This is why Allen ul-timately compares flip-flopping back and forth between being aware of the film as a representation and experiencing it as a projective illusion to the duck-rabbit figure, in which we can choose to see the figure as one thing then another. But this analogy is not convincing either, because in the case of the duck-rabbit we are flip-flopping between two different aspects, between seeing the figure as a duck and seeing it as a rabbit. There is no illusion involved at all, and we see that it is a representation the entire time. Ultimately, Allen is unable to point to any visual experience in which we choose to see something as an illusion or not, and this is because an illusion is not something we can choose to experience.[23]

Allen's misuse of the concept of illusion is also evident in his argument that "our awareness of [a] painting as a painting may be eclipsed entirely, and we may imagine or visualize that the object of the painting is before us, un-mediated by representation."[24] But to visualize or imagine seeing something is not to experience a perceptual illusion in which we see what it is that we are imagining. For unless we are hallucinating, which we also cannot choose to do, imagining seeing something will not create a visual illusion any more than willing it to occur will (although we can of course imagine that we are experiencing a visual illusion). Allen's argument fails because he erroneously conceives of an illusion as something we can choose to experience.

Like theorists in the revelationist tradition, Allen misuses perceptual and related concepts. Unlike them, he does not distrust sight, or subscribe to the revelationist conception of the cinema. As I have shown, despite appearances to the contrary, it was the semiotic-psychoanalytical film theorists who renewed these fundamental tenets of the revelationist tradition by couching them within the theories of the day and by turning toward an autotelic conception of art. For them, just as much as their predecessors, the human eye was unreliable, and they arrived at this skeptical argument in much the same way as their predecessors did: by denying human vision the capacity to see something (that a film is a representation, not reality) that it can see perfectly well unaided.

II

Semiotic-psychoanalytical film theory was the dominant film theory in Anglo-American film studies until the mid-1980s. There are, however, other film theories that have emerged since the 1960s, and like semiotic-psychoanalytical film theory, they too have renewed skepticism about vision and the revelationist conception of the cinema, although at the price, once again, of misusing perceptual and related concepts.

Stanley Cavell has proposed a theory that conceives of film in terms of modern philosophical skepticism, the doubt that reality and other minds exist. For the philosophical skeptic, it is not just that our eyes fail to give us knowledge of the true nature of reality, as is the case with theorists in the revelationist tradition. Rather, the eyes, along with our other sense organs and minds, fail to guarantee that there is a reality to know in the first place. Cavell argues that, for a variety of reasons, humans are naturally inclined to be skeptics, especially in the modern world where, he claims, we feel isolated and trapped in our minds. We believe that our consciousness has become "unhinged" from reality, that our subjectivity is now interposed between ourselves and the world so that it, rather than reality, has "become what is present to us."[25] We therefore wish to make reality present to us again, to escape our solipsistic entrapment in subjectivity. Cavell argues that this wish for the presence of reality, for its "presentness," as he sometimes calls it, is satisfied by different artistic mediums in different ways. Film satisfies it in part by way of what he calls the "automatism" of photography. Drawing on some of André Bazin's arguments, Cavell claims that, because its images are manufactured rather than handmade, photography removes "the human agent from the task of reproduction," thereby escaping human subjectivity. Hence, "photography maintains the presentness of the world by accepting our absence" from the production of its images.[26] But we are also absent from films in another way. Films are projected onto a screen, and the screen is, according to Cavell, a barrier. "It screens me from the world it holds—that is, makes me invisible. And it screens that world from me—that is, screens its existence from me. That the projected world does not exist (now) is its only difference from reality."[27] Cavell clarifies this idea by comparing the audience of a film to the audience in of a play.

> The audience in a theater can be defined as those to whom the actors are present while they are not present to the actors. But movies allow the audience to be mechanically absent. The fact that I am invisible and inaudible to the actors, and fixed

in position, no longer needs accounting for; it is not part of a convention I have to comply with. . . . In viewing a movie my helplessness is mechanically assured: I am present not at something happening, which I must confirm, but at something that has happened, which I absorb (like a memory).[28]

Films make reality present to us at the price of our automatic absence from it, our invisibility.

Cavell therefore argues that the cinema reveals reality in the sense that, for those modern human beings in the grip of skepticism, it satisfies the desire to escape human subjectivity and "see the world itself" by making reality present to them in a manner that is free of human subjectivity. But Cavell also suggests that it reveals reality in another, more reflexive sense. As William Rothman and Marian Keane put it, "Movies awaken us to the world's reality and thereby awaken us to the reality of our unnatural condition, a condition in which we have become displaced, have come to displace ourselves, from our natural habitation within the world."[29] Cavell describes this unnatural condition as follows: due to the hold of skepticism, "our natural mode of perception is to view, feeling unseen. We do not so much look at the world as look *out at* it, from behind the self. . . . Viewing a movie makes this condition automatic, takes the responsibility for it out of our hands," because film makes reality present to us by automatically making us invisible to it.[30] By mechanically instantiating this unnatural, skeptical way of relating to the world, films reveal it to us, making us aware of it and potentially awakening us from it. Hence, film is a "moving image of skepticism." It gives us an image of our skeptical relation to the world.

"The reality in a photograph is present to me," Cavell asserts, "while I am not present to it; and a world I know, and see, but to which I am nevertheless not present (through no fault of my subjectivity), is a world past."[31] But how can something that is past be present to me? This is a logical question about the meaning of the concept of being present to someone, not an empirical one. For the very definition of something being present to someone is that it is in the same spatial location as that person at the same time. Someone is present to me at my wedding because she is at the wedding while it is taking place. She is not present to me if she arrived too late to witness it, or left before it occurred. Cavell could argue that it is, precisely, photography that enables something past to be present to someone. However, this would be circular: Cavell would be appealing to the concept of being present to someone to explain photography, and then appealing to photography to explain his aberrant use of the concept of being present to someone. Moreover, however much as we might want it to, having a photograph of a deceased relative at the relative's funeral does not make him present to those of us at his funeral except perhaps in the metaphorical sense that it makes us think of him. Of course it does make sense to talk about a person being present *in* a photograph. But this is not meant in Cavell's sense of being present to those of us viewing the photograph. Rather, it is meant in the sense of being present when the photograph was taken.

A similar confusion obtains in Cavell's use of the concepts of being unseen and invisible. It only makes sense to say that something is unseen or invisible if it could be seen or visible. One slips into a house unseen because one could have been seen but wasn't. Something is invisible because our eyes are not powerful enough to see it, but if they were more powerful, or if we had a technology that augmented their power, it could be seen. But when we watch a film, we are not invisible or unseen to the people in the film as if, were their eyes only stronger, or they had a telescope, or the "barrier" of the screen was removed, they could see us. As Cavell acknowledges, what a film depicts has already happened. By definition, therefore, we can neither be seen or not be seen by those in a film. When looking at a home movie of our parents as children, we, their children, are not unseen or invisible to them for the obvious reason that we weren't alive when the home movie was made. No matter how powerful their eyes were, they could not have seen us. For what direction would they have looked in? Similarly, we do not see future viewers of photographs and films of ourselves because, no matter how powerful our eyes were, we would not be able to see them. For who will these viewers be, and where will they be located when they see these photographs and films of us? The only licit sense in which one can be unseen when watching a film is if one manages to slip in to see it unnoticed by other members of the audience.

Cavell arrives at these arguments by claiming that photographs are "mysterious" because, unlike a recording of a sound which reproduces the sound, "we cannot say that a photograph reproduces a sight (or a look, or an appearance)."[32] Hence, he concludes, photographs are not recordings of reality, at least in the sense that a recording is a reproduction. Instead, they present reality to us in the sense of making it present to the viewer. But while it is true that it makes no sense to speak of a photograph as reproducing the "sight" of an object because objects don't make sights or have sights, it certainly does make sense to say that a photograph reproduces the look or appearance of an object. This is why we often examine photographs to see how things used to look or appear. By examining photographs of President Kennedy arriving in Dallas on November 22, 1963, for example, we can see what he looked like just before his assassination. Furthermore, it makes sense to say that photographs and films record things. One can, for example, record a performance of a play or dance by filming it, as early filmmakers routinely did. One can also record a historical event, as Abraham Zapruder did when he (unintentionally at first) filmed Kennedy's assassination. There is therefore no reason to think that photographs and films are not reproductions or recordings of things just because they cannot be said to reproduce "sights." Much like semiotic-psychoanalytical film theorists in their misuse of the concept of illusion, Cavell is only able to renew skepticism about human vision and the revelationist conception of the cinema by taking considerable liberties with the meanings of the concept of seeing and related concepts such as being invisible, being present, and sights.

Visual skepticism and the revelationist conception also inform another new film theory, which David Bordwell and Charlie Keil have dubbed the modernity thesis.[33] This theory draws on the early writings of Kracauer as well as Walter Benjamin to argue that human vision goes through changes over time, and these changes are reflected in, if not caused by, visual art and culture.

In modernity, which Benjamin saw as beginning around 1850, a new type or mode of perception different from the modes of previous epochs has arisen due to the forces of change at work in modern societies: capitalism, urbanization, industrialization, technological progress, and so on. This mode is characterized above all by distraction: the frequent shifts in attention demanded of people by the overload of visual and aural stimuli typical of modern environments such as cities. Ben Singer, a modernity thesis proponent, puts it this way:

> The gist of the history-of-perception argument is that modernity caused some kind of fundamental change in the human perceptual apparatus, or "sensorium," as Benjamin and others called it. Immersion in the complex, rapid-fire environment of the metropolis and industrial capitalism created a distinctly modern perceptual mode. The city's bombardment of heterogeneous and ephemeral stimuli fostered an edgy, hyperactive, fragmented perceptual encounter with the world.[34]

In contrast, the prevailing mode of perception in the premodern era was one of contemplation. People were able to look at an object without being distracted by competing perceptual stimuli. But this is not possible, or at least is much less probable, in modernity. Jonathan Crary, another modernity thesis advocate, writes: "Perception for Benjamin was acutely temporal and kinetic; he makes clear how modernity subverts even the possibility of a contemplative beholder. There is never a pure access to a single object; vision is always multiple, adjacent to and overlapping with other objects, desires, and vectors."[35]

According to the modernity thesis, the modern, distracted mode of perception both shapes and is shaped by the visual art and culture characteristic of modernity. In particular, the cinema is said to reflect and intensify perceptual distraction through stylistic techniques such as editing and the close-up, which, much like a modern city, overload the viewer with perceptual stimuli, requiring her to shift attention often and thereby shocking her.

As we saw in chapter 1, in his film theory of the 1920s and early 1930s Kracauer argued that the cinema reveals to human beings their otherwise hidden condition of ideological fragmentation in modernity through the distracting perceptual experience it creates for viewers. By forcing viewers to switch attention frequently from one unconnected stimulus to another, their perceptual experience is fragmented, and this reveals to them their condition of ideological fragmentation. "Here, in pure externality, the audience encounters itself; its own reality is revealed in the fragmented sequence of splendid sense impressions. Were this reality to remain hidden from the viewers, they could neither attack nor change it; its disclosure in distraction is therefore of *moral* significance."[36] Tom Gunning has applied this argument to early cinema, which he refers to as "the cinema of attractions": "The sudden, intense, and external satisfaction supplied by the succession of attractions [in early cinema] was recognized by Kracauer as revealing the fragmentation of modern experience. The taste for thrills and spectacle, the particularly modern form of *curiositas* that defines the aesthetic of attractions, is molded by a modern loss of fulfilling experience."[37] And Miriam Hansen has used this theory of distraction to explain one of the appeals of classical narrative cinema in general—namely, that it was "the single most inclusive cultural horizon in which the traumatic effects of modernity were reflected, rejected or disavowed, transmuted or negotiated."[38] Much like revelationist theorists, therefore, these scholars claim that people are unable to see and know an important truth about reality—namely, their condition of ideological fragmentation—and that the cinema reveals it to them through the distracting perceptual experience it creates for its viewers.

Does it make sense, though, to describe the perceptual experience of film as distracting? Is this a correct use of the concept? For although a film could be said to contain different perceptual stimuli much like a modern environment does, these stimuli—its images and sounds—are typically presented sequentially. Hence, film viewing usually consists of watching one thing—the film—change over time. In contrast, the modern environment contains multiple things that simultaneously compete for our attention, which is why it can distract us. Distraction by definition consists of having one's attention drawn away from one thing by another, and in order for this to happen the two things must be present at the same time. The various images and sounds of a film, however, are not standardly co-present because they are presented sequentially, and they therefore cannot compete with each other for the viewer's attention and thereby distract her. Certainly, the images and sounds of a film can be presented simultaneously. Chantal Akerman, for example, converted her fine film *D'est* (1993) at the Jewish Museum in New York City into a video installation, *Bordering on Fiction* (1995), in which different parts of the film were exhibited simultaneously on multiple monitors. However, this is not how *D'est* is normally exhibited, and the same is true of films in general. This is why, when watching a film, viewers are typically looking at and paying attention to a single perceptual stimulus: what is being exhibited on the screen or monitor in front of them. They are not distracted away from this single perceptual stimulus in the way that competing perceptual stimuli in a modern environment distract its inhabitants away from a single perceptual stimulus. Films, in other words, do not usually cause their viewers to look around, switching attention from one perceptual stimulus in one part of the exhibition space to another.

Given that films do not normally consist of different perceptual stimuli presented simultaneously, if filmmakers truly wanted to replicate the perceptual distraction of the modern environment, they would, surely, have to distract viewers away from the film they are watching with perceptual stimuli located on the sides and back of the exhibition space that are unrelated to the film, a fact recognized by Kracauer. In his essay "The Cult of Distraction," Kracauer argues that "the large picture houses in Berlin are places of distraction" because of their architecture and interior design. "The interior design of movie theaters serves one sole purpose: to rivet the viewer's attention to the peripheral. . . . The stimulations of the senses succeed one another with such rapidity that there is no room left between them for even the slightest contemplation."[39] In other words, according to Kracauer, the interior design of movie theaters distracts the viewer, making him switch attention frequently and abruptly from one feature

of the design to the next. Later in the same essay, however, Kracauer acknowledges that such distraction does not actually occur because of "the programs
of the large movie theaters. For even as they summon to distraction, they immediately rob distraction of its meaning by amalgamating the wide range of
effects—which by their nature demand to be isolated from each other—into
an 'artistic' unity. These shows strive to coerce the motley sequence of exter-
nalities into an organic whole."[40] Although Kracauer does not explain how this
"organic unity" is achieved, one might hypothesize that he is referring to the
fact that theater managers do things such as turn down the lights in order to
minimize the distraction of interior décor, enabling their patrons to concentrate
on the film. But however it is achieved, Kracauer is acknowledging that films
and the exhibition spaces in which they are shown are typically designed to
minimize distraction, not maximize it. Indeed, he ends his essay by complaining that distraction is a potential but unrealized possibility of film exhibition:
film theaters "should rid their offerings of all trappings that deprive film of its
rights," he demands, "and must aim radically toward a kind of distraction that
exposes disintegration instead of masking it."[41]

Benjamin in effect concedes that films are not distracting in this way by
arguing that it is the change from one sequentially presented shot to another
that causes distraction. "The distracting element [of film] is . . . primarily tactile," he says, "being based on changes of *place and focus* which periodically
assail the spectator. . . . No sooner has his eye grasped a *scene* than it is already changed."[42] But this is a major concession. For why should the change
from one shot to another be thought of as a form of distraction? Distraction
by definition consists of having one's attention drawn away from one thing by
another, not of watching one thing change. To think that the two are alike is to
confuse two types of change: the subjective change in our visual field as we
switch our attention from one thing to another, and the objective change that
occurs in one thing while we are watching it.

But let us assume, for the sake of argument, that distraction can occur
as a result of watching one thing change. This still does not mean that film is
distracting. Benjamin seems to think that it is because, unlike paintings, films
do not allow us to contemplate their shots for an indefinite length of time. "The
painting invites the spectator to contemplation," he suggests. "Before it the spectator can abandon himself to his associations. Before the movie frame he cannot
do so."[43] But this argument fails to compare like with like. The cinema is a
temporal art form, one that controls the duration of the viewer's experience of
it. Paintings, however, are still images, and they typically cannot control how
long a viewer looks at them. Change—both in the depicted content and the
way that content is depicted—is therefore always a possibility in films, which
it isn't in paintings, and films by definition control the rate at which this change
occurs. In this respect, the cinema is not like painting, but rather temporal art
forms such as ballet, theater, performance art, opera, and music, which also
typically consist of material that changes and which control the rate at which it
changes. Yet these temporal art forms are not considered distracting. A musical
composition, for instance, usually consists of sounds presented sequentially,

with one sound changing into or being replaced by another, but it does not follow from this that music is distracting. Just because we cannot contemplate a sound in a piece of music for as long as we want to does not mean that we are distracted away from it by the sounds that follow it. There is no reason to think, therefore, that film is distracting because we cannot contemplate a shot for as long as we want to. For if this is true of film, then it must be true of all the temporal arts, most of which existed long before modernity. Thus, once again, skepticism about human vision and the revelationist conception of the cinema are being renewed through the misuse of a perceptual concept, in this case the concept of perceptual distraction.

But even if films could distract us, this would not mean that they could thereby reveal to us our hidden condition of ideological fragmentation (if indeed such a condition obtains in modernity). In his early work, Kracauer and his followers seem to think that this revelation occurs because our perceptual experience is like our experience of ideology in that both are fragmented. But it is important to remember that the word "fragmentation" is a metaphor in both the perceptual and the ideological contexts. When we describe our perceptual experience as "fragmented" (if indeed we ever do), we do not mean that it really is separated into fragments in the way that a film is separated into shots, as we saw in the case of Vertov and his claim that our perceptions are disorganized. For we cannot count our perceptions in the way that we can count the number of shots in a film. Rather, we mean that what we see consists of unconnected perceptual stimuli. And when Kracauer describes ideology as fragmented in modernity, he means, as we have seen, that human beings lack "binding norms." They do not share the common beliefs and values once provided by religion. Thus, perceptual and ideological fragmentation are not really alike. To not share a belief or value with someone else is not in any way like shifting attention frequently and abruptly from one perceptual stimulus to another unrelated one. There is no reason, therefore, to think that the experience of the latter, even if it did routinely occur in the cinema, would lead to the revelation of the former.

One final film theory that has emerged recently and is strongly influenced by skepticism about sight and the revelationist conception is that of Gilles Deleuze, which is based, like his philosophy in general, on Bergson's metaphysics. As we saw in chapter 1 when examining Epstein's work, according to Bergson reality is an indivisible, continuous whole in which everything is constantly interacting with everything else throughout time and space, a process he refers to as mobility. Due to practical necessity, human perception is immobile, subtracting what is seen from its spatial and temporal connections to everything else. Deleuze, like Epstein, bases his film theory on this claim about the gap between reality and the way it appears to human sight. However, again like Epstein, he departs from Bergson's philosophy by arguing that, rather than replicating the immobility of human vision, the cinema overcomes it, thereby revealing the mobility of reality to the viewer. Although he never explains how, the cinema, he insists, does not artificially construct an imitation of movement, as does human perception. Rather, movement is an "immediate given" of the cinematic image, and he therefore calls it a "movement-image."[44] Furthermore,

while framing does subtract what it frames from its spatial and temporal connections to the rest of reality, much like human sight, this is counteracted by
camera movement and editing which, by revealing what is excluded by the
frame, restore these spatial and temporal connections. "If the cinema does *not*
have natural subjective perception as its model, it is because the mobility of its
centres and the variability of its framings always lead it to restore vast acentered
and deframed zones. It then tends to return to the first regime of the movement-
image: universal variation, total, objective, and diffuse perception."[45] Hence, the
cinema oscillates between revealing and hiding the mobility of reality, between
an objective, "acentered" perception, in which what is framed at any one moment is connected to the rest of reality by camera movement and editing, and a
subjective, "unicentered" perception, in which what is framed is separated from
its spatial and temporal connections to the rest of reality.[46]

The real focus of Deleuze's theory, however, is time. Deleuze does not
argue that revealing the mobility of reality automatically entails revealing time
as duration, as Epstein tends to. Rather, he claims that this only comes about due
to a change that occurs in the cinema after World War II. In the pre-war classical
cinema of the movement-image, reality is conceived of as ordered, intelligible,
and predictable. The connections established by camera movement and editing
between what is depicted in one frame and the next are therefore rational and
continuous. One consequence of this is that the cinema can only offer an "indi-
rect image of time," meaning time in the transcendental, Bergsonian sense of a
ceaselessly changing whole in which past, present, and future interpenetrate. In
the classical cinema, this whole is subordinated to space because it is depicted
spatially, through the addition of more and more frames, shots, and scenes.
Hence, time as duration has to be deduced from these spatial additions.[47] The
trauma of WWII, however, "greatly increased the situations which we no longer
know how to react to, in spaces which we no longer know how to describe," and
a modern cinema emerges in which irrational, discontinuous relations between
frames, shots, and scenes predominate, thereby creating ambiguity, paradox,
and even incommensurability.[48] The clear distinctions typical of classical cinema between different times and spaces, subjectivity and objectivity, and real
and imaginary, break down. The result is a "direct image of time": the nonchronological temporal relations that govern modern cinema are those of time
as duration in which the past, present, and future coexist and intermingle. Past
becomes present, present becomes past, and both become future in an image of
time that Deleuze calls "crystalline" because it is multifaceted.

> What we see in the crystal is no longer the empirical progression of time as suc-
> cession of presents, nor its indirect representation as interval or as whole; it is its
> direct presentation, its constitutive dividing in two into a present which is passing
> and a past which is preserved, the strict contemporaneity of the present with the
> past that it will be, of the past with the present that it has been. . . . The direct time-
> image or the transcendental form of time is what we see in the crystal.[49]

Deleuze turns to the films of Alain Resnais to illustrate this argument.

Narration will consist of the distribution of different presents to different characters, so that each forms a combination that is plausible and possible in itself, but
where all of them together are "incompossible," and where the inexplicable is
thereby maintained and created. In *Last Year [at Marienbad],* it is X who knew
A (so A does not remember or is lying), and it is A who does not know X (so X
is mistaken or playing a trick on her). Ultimately, the three characters correspond
to the three different presents . . . : what X lives in a present of past, A lives in a
present of future, so that the difference exudes or assumes a present of present (the
third, the husband), all implicated in each other.[50]

Hence, for Deleuze, like Epstein before him, the cinema is able to grasp and
reveal time as duration, which human perception cannot see because of its immobility, but only when films employing nonchronological temporal relations
emerge after WWII.[51]

As we saw in chapter 1, Bergson has a very broad definition of perception,
arguing that something perceives something else merely by interacting with
it. Deleuze accepts this definition unquestioningly, claiming at one point that
atoms perceive, and indeed that they can perceive more than we humans can![52]
But perceiving does not simply consist of the interaction between one thing
and another. We do not say that a mirror, for example, perceives its environment simply because light rays from the objects around it are reflected on its
surface. Rather, we say that something perceives on the basis of its behavior in
appropriate circumstances, whether it can, for example, discriminate between
or react to perceptual stimuli such as light and dark. As Wittgenstein pointed
out, "Only of a living human being and what resembles (behaves like) a living
human being can one say: it has sensations; it sees; is blind; hears; is deaf; is
conscious or unconscious."[53] It is nonsensical to claim that atoms and mirrors
perceive, because they do not behave like sighted creatures such as ourselves,
let alone have perceptual organs with which to see.

As a result of this broad definition of perception, Deleuze often writes
about the cinema as if it can perceive, as in the quotation above, or as if it is
conscious, as in the following passage: "Given that it is a consciousness which
carries out these divisions and reunions, we can say of the shot that it acts like a
consciousness. But the sole cinematographic consciousness is not us, the spectator, nor the hero; it is the camera—sometimes human, sometimes inhuman
or superhuman."[54] But even though a shot might be like human perception (as
defined by Bergson) in that it separates what it frames from the rest of reality,
this does not mean that it *is* a perception, or that the movie camera perceives
and is conscious. For a camera cannot behave like a sighted or conscious creature. It cannot recognize or fail to recognize an object, identify it or misidentify
it, discover it or overlook it, pay attention to it or ignore it, watch it, observe it,
scrutinize it, study it, or inspect it. Nor can it go blind or lose consciousness.
The camera can certainly help us do some of these things by recording and
thereby enabling us to see what we would not be able to see otherwise. But
this does not mean that the camera performs these actions. In effect, by literal-
izing the analogy between cinema and perception in Bergson's work, Deleuze

traffics in the category confusion between ability and agent that I pointed to in the introduction. Seeing is an ability, something that is identified by its exercise in appropriate circumstances. The cinema can be thought of as a vehicle of sight, something that enables us to see things we would not be able to see otherwise via recordings of them. But this does not mean that it is the cinema that does the seeing for us, as Deleuze suggests. Nor is a shot a perception, if by a perception is meant the subjective content of an act of perception. For although a shot, like a perception, contains information, what makes a perception a perception is that the information it contains is perceived. To contain information is to be in a certain state, while to perceive something is an ability.[55] A photograph, for example, contains information, but it does not perceive this information. Nor, therefore, does a shot, which, after all, is only a series of photographs (whether captured analogically or digitally) exhibited on a screen.

For Deleuze, the post-WWII modern cinema directly reveals time as duration, which the naked eye is incapable of seeing. But as I noted when examining Epstein's work in chapter 1, the dimension of time is not something that, logically speaking, can be seen, and thus the eye cannot intelligibly be accused of failing to see it. The fact that we use time as a noun, Wittgenstein pointed out, misleads us into thinking that it refers to an entity of some kind, like a river flowing by. The phrase "an image of time" therefore seems to make sense, just as "an image of Jupiter" does. But whereas we can point to Jupiter in an image that depicts it, as well as see what shape and color it is, we cannot do the same with time. Hence, there cannot be an image of time, at least in the sense of an image that depicts time. An image can, of course, depict events happening *in* time. But this no more means that it depicts events happening inside some thing that can be revealed, pointed to, and described than an image depicting somebody in love does.

It is not surprising, therefore, that when Deleuze gives examples of what he means by an image of time, it is not something *in* the cinematic image that he points to, because there is nothing he could point to. Instead, he refers to the temporal relations between things in films. As he puts it, "What is specific to the [cinematic] image . . . is to make perceptible, to make visible relationships of time which cannot be seen in the represented object."[56] But as we saw in the case of Vertov, a relation between object A and object B is not an invisible property of object A (or B) that our eyes are too weak to see and that needs to be revealed by a visual technology in order to be seen, as Deleuze suggests in the above quotation. For no matter how powerful our eyes were, we would not be able to see how object A relates to object B simply by looking at object A alone. Instead, by definition, seeing a relation between one object and another consists of seeing both of them and how they stand in relation to each other. The spatial relation of town A being north of town B is not an invisible property of town A which, if our eyes were only more powerful, we would be able to see by looking at town A. Rather, one can only see that town A is north of town B by seeing both towns and their positions relative to each other.

The same is true of temporal relations. As Gregory Currie has pointed out, the cinema is a temporal art in the strong sense that the temporal properties of cinematic representations, such as the order and duration of shots, can represent the temporal properties of what they depict, unlike, say, paintings, which have to use spatial properties such as blurring and positioning to represent the temporal properties of what they depict, as in Duchamp's *Nude Descending a Staircase* (1912).[57] The temporal relation of event B taking place after event A in a narrative film is typically represented by presenting the shots depicting event B to the viewer after the shots depicting event A. In the narrative of *Cléo from 5 to 7* (1961), Cléo meets the young solider on leave from fighting in Algeria in the park at around 6:10 PM after she has broken her mirror at about 6:04 PM, and this temporal relation is represented by shots of her meeting the soldier after the shots of the mirror breaking. No matter how powerful our eyes are, or how powerful the visual technology we have at our disposal, we would not be able to see this temporal relation simply by looking at the shots of her breaking her mirror. As with other kinds of relations, it can only be seen by seeing both events and how they stand in relation to each other temporally. The cinema does not, therefore, represent the temporal relations between two or more things by revealing an otherwise invisible property of those things, as Deleuze argues. Instead, it manipulates its temporal properties, such as the order and length of shots, as well as employs nontemporal techniques, such as titles, to represent temporal relations.

Of course, a film can hide temporal relations. Michael Gondry and Charlie Kaufman, for example, hide the fact that the opening, precredit shots of *The Eternal Sunshine of the Spotless Mind* (2005), in which Joel and Clementine appear to meet for the first time in Montauk, depict an event that actually takes place after the events depicted in the postcredits shots, in which they break up and have their memories of each other erased. But this is not accomplished by making the temporal relation between these events invisible. Instead, it is achieved by presenting the shots that depict these events nonchronologically without informing the viewer that this is being done. The cinema does not, therefore, reveal time which the human eye cannot see. Not only is it senseless to conceive of time as something that can or cannot be seen, but the temporal relations between things that can be seen in films are not invisible properties of those things that need to be revealed by a visual technology. Deleuze, like Vertov, in effect hypostatizes a relational property, conceiving of time as if it were like an intrinsic physical property of a thing that the eye is incapable of perceiving unaided rather than something possessed by virtue of its interaction with other things. In arguing that the cinema is more mobile than human sight, he also follows Vertov in conflating the instantaneous transition that is possible when exhibiting shots recorded at different times and places with the act of recording them to make it seem as if the camera can move instantaneously between different times and places. But as I noted in chapter 2, the camera is no more mobile than the human eye, for it cannot move backward and forward in time. Nor can it move instantaneously between one place and another. Indeed, it cannot move at all—it has to *be* moved. Nor does some kind of instantaneous movement through time and space occur when a viewer is watching a film. For what the viewer sees are shots exhibited in the exhibition space in the present. The fact that these shots were recorded in different times and places does not mean that the shots are moving between these different times and places as the viewer watches them, as Deleuze seems to think.

As I noted in the introduction, one way of defending Deleuze and the other film theorists I have examined in this book against my criticisms is to argue that I am interpreting them too literally, that in fact talk of cameras seeing, or film as being distracting, or the cinematic image making its referent present or being an illusion, is metaphorical. Of course theorists don't believe that these things are literally true of the cinema, someone might protest. However, as I have already pointed out, if this were the case with theorists in the revelationist tradition proper, then they would not arrive at the conclusions that they do about the cinema, and the same is true of the contemporary film theorists I have examined in this chapter. If semiotic-psychoanalytic film theorists, for example, were not claiming that the cinematic image is really illusory but only like an illusion, they would not also argue that it dupes the film viewer into believing that she is in the presence of reality and is an autonomous subject, for if the cinematic image is not literally an illusion then, by definition, it does not deceive the viewer. Nor, therefore, would they impute to it the pernicious political consequences that they tend to. And if Cavell did not believe that the cinematic image really makes its referent present, he would not in addition claim that it satisfies the desire to "see the world itself" and thereby escape human subjectivity, for the film viewer would not be seeing the world, only a recording of it. In the case of the modernity thesis, if it was being suggested that the perceptual experience of film is not really distracting, but only like a distracting perceptual experience, then it would not further be maintained that the cinema contributes to the creation of a new, modern mode of perception in the way that the perceptually distracting modern environment supposedly does, for the simple reason that film would not be literally distracting in the way that modern environments are. And if Deleuze were not arguing that the cinema offers an "image of time," but only something like an image of time (whatever that might be), he would not also claim that the cinema reveals the mobility of reality—in which everything is connected to everything else throughout time and space—because the past and the future would not be literally made present to the viewer in a film.[58] The retreat to suggesting that the claims of film theorists are mere metaphors is always a possibility. But with it must come the recognition that if the claims of film theorists are not literal ones, then neither are the conclusions built on them. Furthermore, it must be explained why film theorists would arrive at those conclusions in the first place if their arguments about the cinema are not meant literally, and what the purpose of such metaphors is if not to make literal claims about the cinema's nature and functions.

That Deleuze draws the conclusions he does from his assertions about the failings of human sight and the cinema's revelatory capacity is ample evidence that he means them literally and that they are therefore open to the sort of criticisms I have leveled against them. Of course, he is far from being alone among film theorists in the way he misuses perceptual concepts to make these arguments. As this book has shown, such misuse has been a persistent tendency in film theorizing since the 1920s. It is time, now, to ask why.

4

The Lure of Visual Skepticism

I

A distrust of human vision has played a foundational role in film theory. It helped give rise to the revelationist tradition within classical film theory and has continued to inform film theorizing since the 1960s. Where does this visual skepticism come from, and what explains its enduring appeal to film theorists?

The answer can be found in artistic modernism where, as much recent scholarship in art history and other disciplines has demonstrated, there is a marked distrust of sight. Rosalind Krauss, for example, has argued that there is a reaction among certain avant-garde artists from the 1920s onward against an idealization of vision that, she believes, is a feature of much modernist art, especially abstract painting and sculpture.[1] By an idealization of vision, Krauss means that much modernist abstract art is designed to give the viewer the experience of "a higher, more formal order of vision" than everyday sight, an experience of vision "in its reflexive form: the terms not just of seeing but of consciousness accounting for the fact of its seeing. It is the axis of a redoubled vision: of a seeing and a knowing that one sees, a kind of *cogito* of vision."[2] The avant-garde counter-tradition of the "optical unconscious" consists of artistic practices that in some way challenge this idealization of vision by inserting non- or anti-ideal features into art works and the viewer's perceptual experience of them, such as time, opacity, and the body. For example, according to Krauss, Max Ernst's collages and readymades challenge the idealization of vision in modernist abstract art by way of a "blind spot," "a break in the field of vision," "a point in the optical system where what is thought to be visible will never appear."[3]

Martin Jay agrees with Krauss that, in France at least, this avant-garde counter-tradition was in full swing in the 1920s. However, he argues that it was part of a much larger but generally ignored "antivisual" or "antiocular-centric" discourse, "a profound suspicion of vision and its hegemonic role in the modern era." This discourse encompassed a variety of intellectual, artistic, and social practices in France and elsewhere from the late nineteenth century onward and was aimed at a widespread valorization of vision in modernity he calls "ocularcentrism" or "Cartesian perspectivalism."[4] Antiocularcentrism is therefore a more pervasive phenomenon than the avant-garde reaction against the idealization of vision in modernist abstract art that Krauss is concerned with. Indeed, according to Jay, certain abstract and semiabstract modernist artists, especially Impressionists and post-Impressionists such as Cézanne, are part of antiocularcentrism, if only ambivalently.[5]

Jonathan Crary also argues that there was a shift in the latter half of the nineteenth century away from the valorization of vision that Jay claims is a major feature of modernity. However, Crary conceives of this shift as being even more widespread and fundamental than Jay's antiocularcentrism. Rather than an early modern valorization of vision that is then increasingly contested, Crary argues that there was a large-scale change in the middle of the nineteenth century in the very concepts used in discourses about visual perception, at least in European countries. Visual perception was no longer conceptualized as a transparent, "decorporealized," and therefore reliable source of information about reality, as it supposedly was prior to the nineteenth cenutry.[6] Rather, "there is an irreversible clouding over of the transparency of the subject-as-observer. Vision, rather than a privileged form of knowing, becomes itself an object of knowledge."[7] For Crary, the shift from a valorization of sight's capacity to attain knowledge of reality to a more skeptical, antirealist conception of visual perception is a big, even epochal change that occurred on the conceptual level, one which effected a wide variety of phenomena, including modernist art.

I suspect that modernity is such a vast and complex phenomenon that generalizations about it of the sort that Jay and Crary advance are implausible. It seems unlikely that any historical epoch can be characterized as having a prevailing view or conception of vision. For example, if one examines the philosophical theories of vision that have been advanced since the nineteenth century, one finds an enormous range of views from realism to antirealism that defy simple generalizations such as "ocularcentric" and "antiocularcentric."[8] Nevertheless, the work of these scholars has helped draw attention to the existence of a distrust of human vision within *artistic* modernism.[9] And while it might be possible to define the nature and scope of this distrust in other ways, the evidence suggests that it can be minimally construed as follows.

There is a specific kind of skepticism about human vision that can be found in artistic modernism in general. It is not confined to Krauss's avant-garde counter-tradition and its reaction against modernist abstraction, nor to Jay's antiocularcentric artistic movements such as Impressionism. Rather, it is a common feature of artistic modernism *in toto,* including those ocularcentric traditions of modernist abstraction that supposedly idealize vision. It is a general, systematic doubt about normal human vision, a distrust of everyday sight. It is a belief that the standard exercise of the visual faculty is not to be trusted in some significant respect because it possesses one or more flaws. By words such as "normal" and "standard," I mean the exercise of the visual faculty outside of artistic contexts in everyday life. Often, this skepticism about normal vision takes the form of the explicitly epistemic claim that humans are unable to see, under standard conditions with their bodily eyes, various truths about reality that it is important to know about, according to modernists. However, even in the absence of such an explicitly epistemic claim, modernists have doubts about everyday sight for a variety of other reasons. Of course, they differ considerably over why normal vision is to be doubted, as well as what the consequences of its inadequacies are. Nevertheless, they overwhelmingly agree that standard, everyday, normal, physical vision is flawed in some crucial respect and therefore cannot be trusted.

P. Adams Sitney has also recently argued that questioning vision is a very common if not essential feature of artistic modernism. He suggests that modernism can be defined as a group of contradictory beliefs or "antinomies" that modernist artists share. A well-known example is the belief that "innovation is the sole legitimate means of guaranteeing [an artist's] link to tradition," a belief which gives rise to the seemingly contradictory practice of "min[ing] the greatest works of [a] tradition" for norms and conventions that can be used to create radically new and innovative art works.[10] A less well-known but equally pervasive contradictory belief is the "antinomy of vision," which Sitney describes as follows: "Modernist literary and cinematic works stress vision as a privileged mode of perception, even of revelation, while at the same time cultivating opacity and questioning the primacy of the visual world."[11] Modernist art works, for Sitney, can be interpreted as allegories of an oscillation between visual opacity and revelation, in which "dramatic moments of vision occur . . . in which nothing, or nothing dramatic, is seen."[12]

Although Sitney does not define the "questioning of the primacy of the visual world" in modernism in the way I have done—as a skepticism about the normal exercise of the visual faculty—he does argue that a questioning of some kind is a very general feature of modernism. And I think that if we remind ourselves of the basic modernist conception of art, as well as of some of the arguments about the inadequacies of normal vision widely appealed to by modernists to justify this conception, we can see how pervasive skepticism about everyday sight is in artistic modernism.

The basic modernist conception of art that I am referring to—one which surfaces in one form or another in almost all modernist theory and practice—argues that genuine art should not imitate or copy the way that reality standardly appears to human vision. Rather, it should be free from the normal exercise of the visual faculty. The artist should transform or abandon the way that reality usually appears to everyday sight; he or she should not slavishly copy it.

As scholars of modernism routinely point out, almost all modernist theories and practices owe some kind of debt to this antirealist or antimimetic conception of art. Rarely noted, however, is the animus against everyday sight motivating this conception, which takes the form of the argument that genuine art should escape from the way that reality standardly appears to it. Modernists differ considerably, however, over *why* art should do this, appealing to many different, relatively informal arguments about the inadequacies of normal vision to justify their practices.

A common example of such an argument is what can be called the "automation of perception" theory. Roman Jakobson provides a classic formulation of it in his early celebration of Futurist painting. Arguing that twentieth-century painting has broken with the "naïve realism" of the nineteenth century, which he defines as the obligation "to convey perception," he claims:

> Perceptions, in multiplying, become mechanized; objects, not being perceived, are taken on faith. Painting battles against the automization of perception; it signals the object. But, having become antiquated, artistic forms are also perceived on faith. Cubism and Futurism widely use the device of impeded perception, which corresponds in poetry to the step-ladder construction discovered by contemporary theoreticians.[13]

The argument that art should "battle against the automization of perception," that it should break with the way that reality standardly appears to everyday sight through the "device of impeded perception," is repeated in a variety of different ways and forms throughout modernist theory and practice and in relation to all the arts. Well-known examples are Victor Shklovsky's theory of *ostranenie* in literature and Bertolt Brecht's theory of *Verfremdung* in theater. So is the argument that Jakobson only hints at here—namely, that the depiction of reality found in genuine art is more truthful and accurate than the way it appears to everyday sight ("painting . . . signals the object"). In other words, through the device of impeded perception, genuine art gets closer than normal vision to true reality.

What is important here about the automation of perception theory is that it perfectly exemplifies modernist distrust of normal vision. In this theory, this distrust takes the form of the argument that the everyday exercise of the visual faculty is characterized by routinization and habituation to the extent that human beings are not actively conscious of much of what they see. As some influential commentators on Shklovsky have put it:

> Normally our perceptions are "automatic," which is another way of saying that they are minimal. From this standpoint, learning is largely a matter of learning to ignore. We have not really learned to drive an automobile, for example, until we are able to react to the relevant stoplights, pedestrians, other motorists, road conditions, and so on, with a minimum of conscious effort. Eventually, we may even react properly without actually noticing what we are reacting to—we miss the pedestrian but fail to see what he looks like. . . . Since perception is usually too automatic, art develops a variety of techniques to impede perception or, at least, to call attention to themselves.[14]

Art, in other words, compensates for a supposed inherent limitation of everyday sight—its tendency to habituate—by impeding this tendency and making people attend to things that they usually overlook. Needless to say, for modernists who subscribe to this theory, it is very important that at least some of the time people be made conscious of what they normally miss due to habituation, even though modernists differ over why this is important. The crucial point here is the distrust of everyday sight that this widely used justification for modernist art is premised on. Normal vision misses a lot; art helps us see more and better.

Another common modernist argument in favor of abandoning the way reality standardly appears to normal human vision in art is what I call the "modern environment" theory, which we have already encountered in the guise of the modernity thesis in chapter 3, and which tends to be confined to the visual arts. According to this theory, the problem with normal human vision is that it is out of sync with the modern environment. Vision is historically outmoded because it is no longer suited to the modern world. Various forces from the mid-nineteenth century onward, principally technology and capitalism, have combined to produce a perceptually challenging environment, particularly in urban centers, one which gives rise to a new visual experience characterized by qualities such as distraction and shock. This visual experience will increasingly become the norm in the modern world, according to the modern environment theory, one which people will have to get used to in order to continue to navigate their environment successfully. What was before thought of as normal human vision, namely contemplation, the ability to look at and think about an object without being shocked and distracted by competing perceptual stimuli, is no longer the norm, but an outdated, old-fashioned, premodern way of seeing. Artists should therefore abandon vision-as-contemplation and instead in some manner address the new visual experience increasingly more typical of modernity.

This theory can be used in various ways. The version of it most familiar today is Walter Benjamin's.[15] Benjamin is usually interpreted as arguing that human beings are undergoing a perceptual change in modernity, one in which their visual faculty is adapting to ("internalizing") the perceptually challenging modern environment. Certain types of art, including film, are playing a role in this historical process by employing formal features that instantiate the shock and distraction that are increasingly becoming norms of visual experience for more and more people. However, Benjamin's is not the only version of the modern environment theory. Another prominent one among modernists, usually overlooked today because of Benjamin's influence, adopts the opposite position. According to this version, because the perceptually challenging modern environment gives rise to a visual experience quite different from that of the premodern period, and because human beings have not had time to adapt to it, art should step in and compensate for the fact that normal human vision is ill-equipped for modernity. Rather than arguing, like Benjamin, that human vision is changing due to the modern environment and that art is playing a role in this process, this version of the theory suggests that art should compensate for the inability of human vision to change.

An excellent example of this latter argument can be found in Fernand Léger's writings from around 1924, during the period of his embrace of the classicism prevalent among the avant-garde in post–World War I Paris.[16] Whereas before this time Léger's argument had been closer to Benjamin's, by 1924, the shock and distraction associated by many modernists with the modern environment are emerging in his writings as unnatural and damaging features of modernity, ones which normal human vision is ill-equipped to deal with. In a text from 1924 titled "The Spectacle: Light, Color, Moving Image, Object-Spectacle," we find him repeatedly criticizing these features. For example, he claims: "The visual world of a large modern city, that vast spectacle that I spoke of in the beginning, is badly orchestrated; in fact, not orchestrated at all. The intensity of the street shatters our nerves and drives us crazy."[17]

Rather than arguing, like Benjamin, that this "overdynamic exterior environment" is being imitated or instantiated by art, Léger now sees it as something that art needs to protect people against. And by 1924 he has come to view a classical ideal of beauty, with its emphasis on harmony and order, as a perfect way of accomplishing this: "If the spectacle offers intensity, a street, a city, a factory ought to offer an obvious plastic serenity. Let's organize exterior life in its domain: form, color, light. . . . A society without frenzy, calm, ordered, knowing how to live naturally within the Beautiful without exclamation or romanticism."[18] Art, in other words, can organize the visual chaos of the modern environment into the geometrical order of "the Beautiful," one which is much more hospitable to everyday sight. Art thereby alleviates the most deleterious effects of the modern environment on the eyes.

Although a lot more can be said about these arguments, what is important here about the modern environment theory is, again, the lack of trust it evinces in normal human vision. For theorists like Benjamin and artists like Léger, everyday sight (viz., the exercise of the visual faculty typical of the premodern period) is ill-equipped to deal with the modern environment. It cannot be relied on in modernity. Art therefore needs to address its historical limitations in some way. For Benjamin, advanced art reflects the new visual features of modernity, thereby playing a role in the process of adapting to the modern environment. For Léger, art should compensate for the eye's inability to adapt by protecting it from these features. But in both cases, art can no longer simply represent the way reality standardly appeared to the visual faculty before the modern era. Art somehow needs to address the fact that normal human vision is historically out of sync with the modern environment.

Yet another common modernist argument in favor of abandoning the way reality standardly appears to normal human vision in art is the modern subjectivity theory discussed in chapter 2. It resembles the automation of perception theory in many ways, but like the modern environment theory, it explicitly ties the inadequacies of the human eye to the historical phenomenon of modernity. As we have seen, this theory argues that various forces in modernity—principally science, technology, and the penetration of "instrumental reason" into all spheres of human existence—have had a profound effect on humans. These forces have altered the way that the average person's mind works, giving rise to a distinctively modern form of consciousness that is overly rationalistic and intrinsically divorced from the senses, the body, and nature in general.

Clearly, this theory evinces a deep skepticism about the normal exercise of the visual faculty, seeing it as part of a modern consciousness enslaved to rational, instrumental imperatives. Humans have lost the capacity to gain purely visual knowledge of reality in modernity. They can no longer see, in the fullest sense of the word. However, as usual, this theory leaves the door open for art to step in and compensate for the flaws of normal vision in a number of different ways. Artists can, for example, abandon normal vision entirely and turn to other resources to attain visual knowledge free from the constraints of rationalistic consciousness. A standard candidate for such a resource is a visionary mental faculty supposedly uncontaminated by instrumental reason—namely, the imagination or the "inward eye." This is a strategy, argues M. H. Abrams, that many Romantics pursued.

> The preoccupation is with a radical opposition in ways of seeing the world, and the need to turn from one way to the other, which is very difficult, but works wonders. "Single vision," the reliance on the "bodily," "physical," "vegetable," "corporeal," or "outward eye," which results in a slavery of the mind to merely material objects, a spiritual sleep of death, and a sensual death-in-life—to this way of seeing [Romantic] poets opposed the liberated, creative, and resurrective mode of sight "thro' and not with the eye," the "intellectual eye," the "imaginative eye," or simply, "the imagination." The shift is from physical optics to what Carlyle in the title of one of his essays called "Spiritual Optics," and what Blake and others often called "Vision."[19]

Alternatively, artists can pursue the option hinted at by Rudolf Arnheim (chapter 2): they can attempt to recapture "undiluted vision" itself—pure, physical sight liberated from the instrumental dictates of the mental realm.

Both strategies, interestingly enough, have been attributed to the film theorist and filmmaker Stan Brakhage, who typically refers to both physical and mental concepts of vision to describe the type of visual experience liberated from an overly rationalistic consciousness that his art aims to capture. For example:

> Suppose the Vision of the saint and the artist to be an increased ability to see— vision. Allow so-called hallucination to enter the realm of perception . . . accept dream visions, day-dreams or night-dreams, as you would so-called real scenes, even allowing that the abstractions which move so dynamically when closed eyelids are pressed are actually perceived. Become aware of the fact that you are not only influenced by the visual phenomenon which you are focused upon and attempt to sound the depths of all visual influence.[20]

William C. Wees has argued that Brakhage is best understood as attempting to capture the undiluted vision of the physical eye freed from the mental. As he puts it, "Brakhage is a literalist of perception, striving to make equivalents of what he sees, as he actually sees it."[21] Others, such as Sitney, have maintained that authentic vision for Brakhage is just as much mental as it is physical.[22] Regardless of which interpretation is right, what is important here is that Brakhage articulates a powerful version of a widespread argument among modernists, which I have called the modern subjectivity theory. And at the center of this theory is the same distrust of normal human vision and the same call to abandon it in art that we have found elsewhere in very different modernist theories of art.

So far, in order to point to the pervasiveness of the distrust of normal human vision that is a common feature of modernism, I have examined several of the most influential but informal arguments about the inadequacies of everyday sight that modernist artists appealed to. However, modernists also routinely turned to more formal philosophical and scientific doctrines to justify their artistic departure from normal vision. Indeed, they were often motivated by such doctrines to produce art in the first place. And, once again, although these doctrines differ considerably in many ways, they all provide plenty of ammunition for the modernist distrust of everyday sight. We have already encountered one of these theories, Bergsonism, but there were others, too.

A good example is the spiritual philosophies of one sort or another that, according to much research in art history, played a crucial role in the development of abstract painting by European painters born from the 1860s onward. Pioneering abstractionists as different as Wassily Kandinsky, Frantisek Kupka, Jean Arp, Piet Mondrian, and Kazimir Malevich all moved toward abstraction due to their desire to represent spiritual ideals. These were culled from a variety of mystical and occult doctrines popularized in the late nineteenth and early twentieth centuries by writers and spiritual leaders such as Alfred Percy, Helena P. Blavatsky, Franz Hartmann, Charles W. Leadbeater, and Rudolf Steiner. And many other abstract, semiabstract, and nonabstract visual artists of their generation were also influenced, to varying degrees, by such philosophies.

It is impossible to summarize all of these spiritual philosophies here. What is important is that, despite their variety, they shared certain basic features described by Maurice Tuchman as "a concern for the quality of inner life, an interest in spiritual development and wholeness, and a mistrust of material values and appearances."[23] And it is the latter antimaterialism that is of particular relevance to the claim that skepticism about normal human vision is a very common feature of modernism. For this general antimaterialism helped give rise to the collective effort in modernist visual art to "transcend the visible," to use Sixten Ringbom's words[24]—to leave behind the way reality appears to the bodily eye and represent instead a higher, more authentic state of insight into, or absorption in, reality through abstract, nonrepresentational styles and forms. At the heart of this antimaterialism is a basic doubt about normal human vision and the way reality appears to it, which here takes the form of a widespread belief, one we encountered in the work of Epstein in chapter 1: that everyday sight and the senses in general are confined to outer material appearances and are usually incapable of perceiving inner spiritual or metaphysical truths.

While explicitly spiritual doctrines were an important influence on experimentation by visual artists during modernism's formative period between 1890 and 1930, ostensibly more materialist philosophies and theories also played a crucial role in promoting doubt about the normal exercise of the visual faculty, theories which either added weight to the ontological gap between appearance and reality at the heart of neoplatonism and other spiritualist doctrines or legitimized a naturalistic version of this gap. One such group of theories, which grew out of developments in early nineteenth-century geometry, popularized the fertile concept of a spatial fourth dimension invisible to the naked human eye. And as Linda Dalrymple Henderson has shown, this concept had a considerable impact on a wide variety of modernists. Although only a few visual artists actively investigated the non-Euclidean geometries from which the concept of a spatial fourth dimension sprang, fastening on to their relativist implications, the concept itself became "a concern common to artists in nearly every major modern movement" from analytical cubism through to Duchamp, Dada, and De Stijl because it supported a plethora of interpretations and styles. These interpretations can be grouped into two basic schools, which in practice often overlapped: one consisting of artists such as Malevich interested in the abstract depiction or evocation of spiritual and metaphysical truths, who saw the fourth dimension as an example of a higher spiritual reality beyond material appearances, and the other consisting of artists such as the Dadaist Tristan Tzara belonging to the nihilist wing of modernism, who employed it in their battle against logic and reason as proof of the relativity and conventionality of rationality and human conceptual schemes in general. However, for both schools, the fourth dimension concept provided yet another reason to be skeptical toward everyday sight, either because of the inability of the bodily eyes to perceive the fourth dimension, or the supposed relativity of the three dimensions they do perceive; as well as yet another impetus for making abstract or semiabstract art. As Henderson puts it, "belief in a fourth dimension encouraged artists to depart from visual reality and to reject completely the one-point perspective system that for centuries had portrayed the world as three-dimensional."[25]

Although the concept of a spatial fourth dimension was eventually replaced in the popular imagination in the 1920s by Einstein's much more scientifically significant temporal fourth dimension, it should be pointed out that the skepticism toward everyday sight that this particular concept generated is a feature of a much broader picture of the natural universe that was put into place by the success of the modern physical sciences from the seventeenth century onward, one which lasts to this day and which we encountered briefly in chapter 1—namely, the doctrine of secondary qualities. Sharing many of the same philosophical sources as neoplatonic and other spiritualist doctrines, this picture legitimizes a naturalistic version of the neoplatonic gap between the way reality appears to human perception and the way reality actually is in its claim that, while the world appears to human beings to be multicolored, noisy, many-scented, and hot or cold, in reality there is only the rapid movement of colorless, noiseless, scentless particles, of waves of air or electromagnetic radiation. Even modernists with only the most superficial grasp of modern science could not have failed to be aware of this striking picture of the natural universe that science had erected. And while the philosophical coherence of the picture has long been disputed, and the picture itself is vague enough to generate a number of respectable philosophical positions between realism and antirealism on perception,[26] it could only help cement skepticism about everyday sight in a modernist context already overdetermined by such skepticism and not aware of, or sophisticated enough to address, the philosophical complexities of this picture.

Thus far, I have surveyed some of the most influential formal and informal theories of the inadequacies of normal human vision used by modernists to justify their artistic departure from everyday sight and the way reality appears to it. While this survey is by no means intended to be exhaustive, I hope that by briefly examining a fairly wide range of influential modernist arguments, I have provided enough evidence to support my contention that a skepticism about the ordinary exercise of the visual faculty is a very common feature of modernism. For most modernists, everyday sight is not to be trusted in some significant respect because of one or more flaws. Normal vision is inauthentic. Modernist art, meanwhile, attempts to compensate for this inauthenticity by partially or wholly departing from the way reality usually appears to everyday sight and finding more authentic "ways of seeing."

This skepticism, I am suggesting, is a widespread feature of modernism, overdetermined by a number of different arguments about the inadequacies of normal human vision that are used to motivate very different, often conflicting, modernist agendas. In other words, it is a prejudice shared by modernists of very different, even antithetical persuasions, much like the belief pointed to by Sitney that "innovation is the sole legitimate means of guaranteeing [an artist's] link to tradition."[27] Indeed, it is broad enough to be shared by ocular-centric artists such as Mondrian, and antiocularcentric artists who are part of the tradition of "optical unconscious" such as Duchamp, to use Jay and Krauss's terminology. For while Mondrian, unlike Duchamp, may well have believed in the possibility of the artistic representation of some kind of neoplatonic reality, such a belief is still predicated on the antiocularcentric assumption that every-day sight is not up to the task of accessing that reality in the first place because it is confined within the earthly, corporeal limitations of opacity, of repetition, of time—the very features of the optical unconscious that, according to Krauss, Duchamp and others foreground in their art. Mondrian and Duchamp, in other words, share a similar conception of the condition of normal human vision, even though they differ considerably about how art should escape this condition and find more authentic ways of seeing. For Mondrian, authenticity consists of neoplatonic essences hidden behind appearances; for Duchamp, if Krauss is right, it consists of self-reflexively foregrounding the condition of everyday sight itself, namely, the optical unconscious. Yet, both basically agree about the nature of this condition.

This skepticism about everyday sight is a very general feature of modern-ism because it functions as a compelling rationale for the purpose of modernist art. Where normal human vision cannot be trusted, modernist art steps in and compensates in some way, helping people see more authentically, often by revealing the truths they normally fail to see. In other words, for modernists in general, a common justification for their art is that it compensates for the inadequacies of everyday sight by providing a more authentic way of seeing to its viewers. It allows people to escape from the limitations of normal vision. Different modernists may believe that there are other ways of helping people see more authentically. But, they overwhelmingly believe that art is one way to achieve this goal, and that without the aid of art at least some of the time, humans are very much in the dark, so to speak.

This rationale is especially powerful in the case of those modernists who make the epistemic argument that human beings are standardly unable to see and know important truths about reality. For this claim creates a coveted role for art: to reveal such truths. This role is highly attractive to artists because it gives the arts considerable status and moral authority, placing them on a par with other truth-seeking pursuits such as philosophy, science, and religion. The philosopher Charles Taylor writes:

> There are strong continuities from the Romantic period, through the Symbolists and many strands of what was loosely called "modernism," right up to the present day. What remains central is the notion of the work of art as issuing from or realizing an "epiphany," to use one of Joyce's words in a somewhat wider sense than his. What I want to capture with this term is just this notion of a work of art as the locus of a manifestation which brings us into the presence of something which is otherwise inaccessible, and which is of the highest moral and spiritual significance.[28]

This is why art is so revered in the modern era, argues Taylor, and why artists are seen as "heroes," "visionaries," "seers," and so forth. Because most people are supposedly limited in their capacity to see and know truths about reality, artists who reveal such truths are viewed as extraordinary, and art, the locus of their revelation, is venerated.

This explains, I think, the attraction of film theorists and filmmakers to skepticism about human vision and the cinema's revelatory capacity, especially first-generation theorists such as Epstein, Vertov, Balázs, and Kracauer, who formulated their theories when modernism was at its height in the 1920s and when the cinema had not yet been widely accepted as an art. Not only did the cinema's revelatory power enable them to differentiate the cinema from the other arts, thereby satisfying the requirement of the doctrine of medium specificity to which they subscribed, but by embracing skepticism about sight and the revelationist conception they could counter detractors by arguing that the cinema has a morally profound role to perform: to reveal important truths about reality that human beings cannot see and know, much like scientists do using visual technologies such as microscopes and telescopes. Film is a vital art, they could claim, because it enables mass enlightenment. This also explains the euphoria of these theorists and filmmakers about the cinema and why, as we saw in the introduction, they combined skepticism about sight, which they inherited from the modernist tradition, with a realist embrace of the cinema's capacity to mechanically record reality. As we have seen, like modernist visual artists in general, they had doubts about sight and wanted to depart from the way reality appears to it in order to reveal otherwise in-accessible truths about reality. The cinema, they believed, fulfilled this role because it can reveal features of reality invisible to the naked eye, just as a painter can depart from the way reality appears to sight through abstraction and other styles. However, a painting is still dependent on the intentions of a human being who, however enlightened, has flawed vision from the perspec-tive of modernist skepticism about sight. In contrast, the cinema is indepen-dent of human intentions, human vision, and human beings, because it is a machine. Those in the revelationist tradition embraced the capacity of film to mechanically record reality because they believed that, in conjunction with the cinema's revelatory power, it offered a way to escape the limitations of the human eye and to see reality as it is.

II

I have argued that film theorists and filmmakers are attracted to skepticism about human vision because it provides a powerful rationale for the purpose of cinematic art, for its role or value. Another possible explanation for this at-traction is that skepticism about sight is valid. Although the specific arguments film theorists have made about vision might be wrong, it could still be that there are good reasons to be skeptical about our perceptual capacities. Don't we often make mistakes in our perceptual judgments concerning how things are in the world? And doesn't this show that our senses are fundamentally unreliable? Furthermore, the cinema can reveal truths about reality invisible to the naked eye, such as the precise position of the legs of galloping horses. Doesn't this confirm the revelationist claim that the cinema escapes the eye's limitations?

The "argument from the notorious limitations and fallibilities of our senses to the impossibility of our getting to know anything by looking, listening and touching" is one that Ryle addressed, and sought to counter, in his classic paper "Perception."[29] Wittgenstein did the same in his investigations into the concepts of doubt and certainty in the unfinished writings that have been collected in the volume *On Certainty.*[30] Although much more space is needed to do justice to this topic, I will briefly survey their major claims. For if these philosophers are right, then there is no good reason to distrust sight, as modernists tend to. To start with, as Wittgenstein pointed out, we cannot act in our everyday lives as if our visual faculty is consistently unreliable, unless it is not functioning correctly. Whatever doubts about vision we might subscribe to in theory, they are impossible to systematically sustain in practice, in our normal behavior. They make little difference to everyday life. If, for example, a skeptic were to doubt the existence of a table despite the fact he could see it, "how would his doubt come out in practice?" asks Wittgenstein. "Couldn't we peacefully leave him to doubt it, since it makes no difference at all?" (OC §120) At most, such doubts might show up some of the time in what a skeptic says and feels, but they would not fundamentally alter the skeptic's behavior (OC §339).

More significant, the concept of doubt cannot be generalized into a sys-tematic doubt of the skeptical variety without becoming unintelligible and un-usable: "A doubt that doubted everything would not be a doubt" (OC §450). Wittgenstein points to this in a number of different ways. Children, for ex-ample, learn words and facts first, and then learn what it means to doubt them. It would be impossible for children to learn anything if doubt was part of their education from the beginning, if, when teaching a child what the word "violet" means by showing him or her a picture of the flower, an adult said, "perhaps that is a violet" (OC §450).

Once the meaning of the concept of doubt and its various applications in practice is learned, background certainties must be in place in order to doubt in-telligibly: "The game of doubting itself presupposes certainty" (OC §115). For example, "If the shopkeeper wanted to investigate each of his apples without any reason, for the sake of being certain about everything, why doesn't he have to investigate the investigation?" (OC §459). The shopkeeper, in other words, has to rely on his investigation in order to investigate his fruit; otherwise he will be forced into the senseless procedure of investigating his investigation of his investigation, and so on. Similarly, in the empirical sciences, "If I make an experiment I do not doubt the existence of the apparatus before my eyes. I have plenty of doubts, but not *that*" (OC §337; emphasis in original). Or in math-ematics, "If I do a calculation I believe, without any doubts, that the figures on the paper aren't switching of their own accord" (OC §337). Practices that in-volve doubt—investigations, experiments, calculations—require background certainties that are taken for granted, such as the existence of the apparatus used to conduct an experiment. If doubt is generalized and these background certainties are questioned, then practices such as experiments that involve doubt are rendered unintelligible and pointless. Indeed, even the most radical skeptic takes something for granted—namely, the meanings of the words he uses to express his skepticism. For if the meanings of these words are doubted, then the skeptic cannot rely on getting them right and therefore cannot express his skepticism: "If you are not certain of any fact, you cannot be certain of the meaning of your words either" (OC §114).

Finally, it is only because of the logical possibility of certainty that, when we have grounds for doing so, it makes sense to doubt something in the first place. In other words, the concept of doubt can only be used meaningfully when certainty is a logical possibility. Take, for example, the question of whether another person is really in pain. A skeptic typically generalizes doubt by arguing that it is impossible to ever know with certainty whether another person is in pain because we may find out that the person in question is not really in pain but is only pretending to be. But, as Wittgenstein labored to show, if it is impossible to know with certainty whether another person is in pain in the present, then it is equally impossible in the future—meaning that it can never be discovered whether the person in question is in pain or only pretending. But this renders the concept of doubt unintelligible. It makes no sense to argue that we can never know with certainty whether another person is in pain because we may discover in the future that he is pretending, if such a discovery is impossible.

I cannot discover in the future that a person is pretending to be in pain if it is impossible for me to ever know with certainty whether someone is in pain or only pretending to be.[31]

As this example shows, doubting whether something is true is logically dependent on the possibility of being certain about whether it is true or not, even if being certain is not always an empirical possibility. The outcome of the skeptic's generalization of doubt, as Wittgenstein pointed out, is not that we cannot know with certainty whether another person is in pain because he may be pretending to be in pain, but that the concept of doubt and related concepts such as pretense become unusable. "But what does it mean to say that all behavior *might* always be pretence? Has experience taught us this? How else can we be instructed about pretense? No, it is a remark about the concept 'pretence.' But then this concept would be unusable, for pretending would have no criteria in behavior."[32] The logical possibility of being certain is part of the meaningful use of the concept of doubt. It is part of the language game of doubting. Without this possibility, doubting becomes unintelligible.

All of this is also true of vision. General, systematic doubt within the context of sight is equally as unintelligible as in other contexts. Doubting and testing what we see is only intelligible against a background of certainties that are taken for granted, such as the existence of our eyes. And it is only because of the logical possibility of being certain of what we see that, when we have grounds for doing so, it makes sense to doubt it. We doubt what we see because we can then, for example, go back and look at it again, or move to see it in a better light or from a better vantage point, or in some other way find out the truth about it: "If e.g. someone says 'I don't know if there's a hand here' he might be told 'Look closer.'—The possibility of satisfying oneself is part of the language-game. Is one of its essential features" (OC §3). It is only because we can potentially satisfy ourselves perceptually that something is the case that we can intelligibly doubt it in the first place. Without this logical possibility, doubting what we see would lose its point. Ryle uses the following example to make this claim:

> You and I sometimes make mistakes in counting, adding and multiplying, and we may remind ourselves of this general liability in the very same breath with making one of these mistakes. So, at first sight, it looks as though we ought to surrender and say that we can never find out by counting the number of chairs in a room and never find out by adding or multiplying the right answers to our arithmetical problems. . . . Very good—but how is the mistake exposed? By someone counting correctly or by someone adding correctly. . . . So far from our thinking that perhaps nothing can ever be found out by counting or adding, we realize not only that things can be so found out but also that among the things that can be thus found out are mistakes in counting and adding.[33]

If philosophers such as Wittgenstein and Ryle are right, sight is not fundamentally unreliable, as modernists and revelationist film theorists and filmmakers tend to argue. Skepticism about human vision is therefore not a solid foundation on which to build theories of film and should be abandoned. Although vision is fallible, the intelligibility of it being so is dependent on the logical possibility that visual oversights and errors can be corrected and that they occur against a background of certainties that are not questioned.

This points to the correct way of conceptualizing the relation between visual technologies and human perception. If it is true that vision is on the whole reliable, then such technologies, while more powerful than the eye in certain respects, do not escape the limitations of human perception. Instead, they *extend* our already existing capacity to see and know the world around us. They *enable* us to see further and know more than we would be able to otherwise. Discovering the particulate structure of an object using a microscope, for example, presupposes that we can see the microscope correctly. It also assumes that we can accurately see what the microscope reveals, and that any mistakes we make in doing so can be corrected by looking through the microscope again, or using another one, or having someone else confirm what we see. Using such technologies, in other words, relies on the fact that our eyes are reliable and that we already can see and know the world around us. If we couldn't, they would be of no help to us, for we would no more be able to see what is the case in our environment with them than without them. Thus, in as much as it is like other visual technologies and does reveal truths about reality that are invisible to human perception, the cinema does not do so by escaping the eye's limitations or developing new perceptual faculties in us, as theorists in the revelationist tradition argue. Rather, it *augments* our already existing capacity to find out about the environment around us using our eyes.[34]

III

I have argued that human sight, even though fallible, is not limited to the extent that theorists in the revelationist tradition claim. Not only is visual skepticism probably incoherent, for the philosophical reasons I have just examined, but most of the truths about reality that the cinema reveals, according to these theorists, are either ones that it makes no sense to accuse the naked human eye of failing to see or ones that it can see just fine unaided. This does not mean, however, that revelationist theorists were wrong to assert that film has greater revelatory powers than the other arts, at least as these other arts were standardly practiced when they formulated their theories. First, cinematic techniques such as time-lapse photography do enable us to see features of reality, such as the precise leg positions of galloping horses, that are invisible in the sense that we are incapable of seeing them without a visual technology due to the limitations of our eyes. Second, and more important, because of their desire to legitimize film as an art by equating it with the scientific discovery of inaccessible features of the natural universe using visual technologies, revelationist theorists overlooked the fact that there are other senses of revelation pertinent to the cinema. Indeed, the comparison between film and other revelatory visual technologies at the heart of the revelationist tradition obscures the ways in which the cinema is uniquely capable of revealing truths about reality. For although this comparison helps differentiate film from the other arts, it does so by assimilating its revelations to those of science. In other words, the cinema's difference from the preestablished arts is purchased at the price of aping pre-existing visual technologies such as microscopes and telescopes. Furthermore, this comparison places the heavy burden on the film theorist of having to show that human vision is incapable of seeing the truths revealed by the cinema, just as it is incapable of seeing distant planets and microbes, a requirement that, as I have demonstrated, often results in a category error. Once we clarify the other senses of revelation of relevance to film art, we can reconstruct the revelationist claim that it allows us "to see more and better" than the other arts in a nonessentialist way that neither sacrifices cinematic specificity nor involves a misuse of our perceptual concepts.

Microscopes, telescopes, and other visual technologies are normally used by scientists to reveal truths about natural phenomena because such phenomena, or parts of them, are invisible in the sense that they are impossible for human beings to see unaided. On the basis of such revelations, scientists form hypotheses about the explanatory principles governing the nature and behavior of such phenomena, which in turn allow them to predict how they will behave in given situations. These hypotheses are open-ended, in that they can be tested against further observations and refined or rejected. And the predictions they give rise to can help humans manipulate the phenomena being investigated to their advantage. For example, by observing asteroids using telescopes, scientists can form hypotheses about how their size, density, and other factors govern the direction and speed of their movements. Such hypotheses allow them to predict their movements in given situations, such as when they collide with other asteroids. When these situations occur and are observed, the underlying hypotheses can be modified or rejected if the predictions they give rise to are wrong. And these predictions potentially enable humans to control asteroids in a way that benefits them, for example by devising technologies that prevent them from colliding with Earth.

Is this the sort of truth about reality that the cinema reveals? Obviously, it can. For example, film and other moving image technologies, when affixed with the requisite lenses, can record the otherwise inaccessible movements of asteroids, thereby helping scientists to explain, predict, and potentially control them. But this is not the only type of revelation that what we call *films* (as opposed to the *technology of film*) usually traffic in. We say, for example, that Peter Parker reveals that he is Spiderman to Mary-Jane Watson in *Spiderman 2* (2004) (fig. 4.1), that David Harris reveals that he killed police officer Wood in *The Thin Blue Line* (1988), and that Marianne reveals that she thinks her father-in-law, Isak Borg, is a selfish, utterly ruthless man in *Wild Strawberries* (1957). But we do not say that these truths are revealed because they were hitherto invisible in the sense of being impossible to see without assistance. Rather, we say that they are revealed because they were previously concealed. As I noted in chapter 2 in the examples of Mae Marsh's hands and the photograph hidden in the desk, in addition to being impossible to see without a

Figure 4.1. Mary Jane Watson after learning that Peter Parker is Spiderman in *Spiderman 2* (Sam Raimi, 2004).

visual technology, to be invisible means to be hidden from view, and things that are deliberately hidden are typically possible to see unaided, otherwise there would be no reason to hide them. This is in contradistinction to things that are impossible to see without assistance, such as microbes, which remain invisible whether they are hidden or not. Hence, the fact that Peter Parker is Spider-man, that David Harris killed Officer Wood, and that Sara thinks poorly of her father-in-law does not need to be revealed by a visual technology in order to be discovered. Rather, these truths are revealed in these films in the way that people typically reveal truths about themselves in real life, through words and behavior, which we are perfectly capable of perceiving without help unless suffering from an impairment.

Films are full of such revelations of previously concealed truths about human beings, which typically occur by way of verbal confessions, behavior which gives them away, or when the film's narration or style informs the viewer of them. Alfred Hitchcock's films, for example, traffic in these latter two modes of revelation. As we shall see, his masterpiece *Shadow of a Doubt* (1943) employs expressionistic stylistic techniques from its opening scene to hint that Uncle Charlie is the so-called merry widow murderer, and Hitchcock often draws the viewer's attention to details of his behavior unseen by other characters that suggest the same. But the fact that he is a murderer is not something that is invisible to these characters and the viewer in the sense that it is impossible to see unaided. Rather it is invisible in the sense that Uncle Charlie conceals it. And it is discovered not by way of visual technologies, but in the way that people usually discover truths about others—through observing his actions and witnessing his confessions.

It might be objected that thoughts, feelings, and many other truths about human beings are internal, mental phenomena and therefore are hidden behind external behavior, much like the internal mechanism of the clock in *The Fall of the House of Usher* is hidden behind its external face. Doesn't this mean that they are invisible to human perception in the same way that microbes and distant planets are? Isn't it the case that our sense of sight is not powerful enough to see beyond the exterior of the face and body into the interior mind, just as it is not strong enough to see microbes or planets a great distance away? No, for as we saw in chapter 2, mental states and events are not intrinsically hidden or private, as the Cartesian myth would have it, for if they were, we would not be able to refer to them intelligibly because there would be no public criteria for the correct use of mental concepts. Instead, we can often see the pain in another person's face or hear it in her voice, or see from her behavior that she is desperately sad or thinking hard. This is because mental phenomena have characteristic behavioral manifestations that function as criteria (as opposed to symptoms) for their presence. Behavior is not a mere external accompaniment to the real mental state or event, which is somewhere internal, invisible to the naked eye like, say, Broca's area. A woman giving birth to a child is not feeling pain somewhere inside her and, in addition, screaming and writhing in agony. Rather, her pain is manifest in her cries and bodily movements. Of course, one can hide one's thoughts, feelings, and much else by concealing them. But this consists of in some way dissimulating their characteristic behavioral expressions. One masks one's sadness by holding back one's tears, or one speaks and acts as if one thinks the opposite of what one really does. The fact that we have to take steps to conceal our thoughts and feelings shows that they are not normally hidden, for if they were we would not have to take such steps. It is true that most of us do not give verbal or physical expression to our mental lives all of the time, and this means that other people cannot always perceive them. But this does not necessarily mean that we are hiding our thoughts and feelings, for we will often tell or show other people what we are thinking or feeling if asked to do so.[35] Hence, it is not a visual technology that is required to perceive the mental lives of others, as a CAT scan is needed to see their brains, but rather access to the words and behavior that manifest those lives.

Revealing what is invisible in the sense of making visible what human perception is incapable of perceiving unaided does, of course, occur in films. And it can coexist with revelation in the sense of making known previously concealed truths that are capable of being perceived without assistance. Crime documentaries often contain footage of forensic evidence, such as hairs and saliva, being subjected to microscopic analysis, which reveals who committed a crime by making visible microscopic particles invisible to human perception, as well as interviews with the criminal in which he reveals that he committed the crime by way of confessions and deeds that can be perceived unaided. Typically, however, when we say that a film (as opposed to the technology of film) reveals something, we mean it in the latter sense much more often than we do in the former, and this is because films are for the most part humanistic in character. While the sciences can and do employ film and other moving image technologies to make discoveries about invisible natural phenomena, what we call films are usually about the visible world of human (or humanlike) agents and their actions, words, identities, thoughts, feelings, wishes, struggles, histories, circumstances, and much else besides, and we are quite capable of perceiving such things unaided. Furthermore, we watch films for the most part because we enjoy stories (whether fictional or not) about other agents, we often learn something about human life from them, and we value the way filmmakers present them to us, the aesthetic choices they make and the creativity manifest in these choices. We do not, on the whole, watch them in order to construct hypotheses about the explanatory principles governing a natural phenomenon that is invisible to us that we want to explain and potentially control, although films can present us with the *results* of scientific research into such phenomena, as Al Gore's *An Inconvenient Truth* (2006) does. The comparison between the cinema and other revelatory visual technologies is therefore a misleading one because it suggests that films "reveal truths about reality" in a scientific sense, allowing viewers to make discoveries about natural phenomena they would otherwise not be able to see in the same way that a scientist does using microscopes and other visual technologies, when it is far more common for films to reveal truths about people that are possible to see unaided but have for some reason been concealed. The phrase "revealing truths about reality" is also potentially deceptive, because it is a "smothering" expression, to use Ryle's term, masking significant logical differences between types of truth, revelation, and invisibility.

It is striking that although theorists in the revelationist tradition compare cinematic revelation to scientific discoveries using visual technologies of inaccessible natural phenomena to differentiate film from the other arts, many of the examples they give involve human beings. Epstein and Balázs, for example, suggest that the cinema can reveal what people are really thinking and feeling in the same way that microscopes and telescopes can bring to view microbes and distant planets. As I have argued, the mind is not invisible in the sense that microbes or distant planets are. It does not require a visual technology in order to be seen, as Epstein and Balázs claim, because we are often able to see what a person is thinking or feeling unaided. Nevertheless, there is an insight about the difference between the cinema and the other visual arts buried in this misleading comparison. For although other visual arts can also reveal cognitive and affective states, films can do so in ways they cannot because, as Noël Carroll has pointed out, they have at their disposal a property that the other visual arts, at least in their customary forms, lack: variable framing. Editing and camera movement enable filmmakers to control the viewer's attention to a much greater degree than is possible in the other visual arts. To use Carroll's terminology, by moving the camera toward an object, editing and camera movement can index it, suggesting to the viewer that he pay attention to it, much like the gesture of pointing. These techniques can also exclude or bracket what surrounds the object, so that the viewer literally cannot pay attention to anything else on screen. And finally, in moving the camera toward an object, its scale is changed as it fills up more screen space, which further suggests that the object should be attended to by the viewer or forces the viewer to do so.[36] Using these techniques, films can direct our attention to details of human behavior that reveal much that might otherwise remain concealed.

Although indexing, bracketing, and scaling are distinct functions of variable framing, in practice they often occur together and reinforce one another. In *Shadow of a Doubt,* just before young Charlie nearly dies of suffocation from exhaust fumes in the garage where her uncle, also named Charlie, has deliberately left the family car running, her family is gathering in the living room to go out for the night. In a medium shot, Uncle Charlie, who has returned to the house having set the deadly trap for his niece, makes small talk with his sister and brother-in-law as they put on their coats (fig. 4.2). He is smiling, and his face has the friendly demeanor he usually employs to mask his true malevolent self. As his niece descends the stairs, the camera dollies in to a medium close-up of him alone (fig. 4.3), thereby indexing and enlarging the scale of his face

Figure 4.2. Uncle Charlie makes small talk with his sister and brother-in-law in *Shadow of a Doubt* (Alfred Hitchcock, 1943).

Figure 4.3. The camera dollies toward Uncle Charlie, bracketing the other characters.

in the shot, and bracketing the rest of the family. His smile fades, and his brow furrows as he looks up at her while the rest of the family continues talking (fig. 4.4). By drawing our attention to this small, momentary change in his facial expression by way of variable framing, Hitchcock is revealing what the family members around him are oblivious to because he conceals it from them: that he is thinking about his plot to kill his niece. We cut to a *plan Américain* of Charlie coming down the stairs as she joins the conversation about who should go in a taxi (there are too many people to fit in the family car) (fig. 4.5). Uncle Charlie, smiling once again, suggests that he and his niece take the car. Hitchcock cuts to a close-up of the girl's wide-eyed face as, for a brief second, it reveals her alarm at the thought of traveling alone with her uncle, whom she knows is trying to murder her (fig. 4.6), once again making use of indexing, bracketing, and scaling. But her smile quickly returns, thereby hiding her true feelings from her family, as the camera dollies back to a two-shot and she turns to her uncle to insist that he go in the taxi while she takes the car (fig. 4.7).

This film, and Hitchcock's films in general, are full of such revelations of what is really going in the minds of characters, often unbeknownst to those around them. They perfectly illustrate the way revelation often occurs in films in the sense of making visible the otherwise concealed cognitive and affective states of human beings by way of variable framing that allows the viewer to closely observe details of their behavior that gives these states away. Nonfiction

Figure 4.4. The shot indexes Uncle Charlie's face and enlarges its scale. As he looks at his niece descending the stairs off-screen, his true thoughts and feelings are revealed in close-up as his smile fades.

Figure 4.5. A *plan Américain* eyeline match of young Charlie descending the stairs.

Figure 4.6. Young Charlie's alarm at the thought of traveling alone with her uncle is momentarily revealed in close-up.

Figure 4.7. Charlie's alarm is quickly concealed behind a smile as the camera dollies back to a two-shot of her and her uncle.

films also use similar techniques for the same reason, such as the close-up of Jackie Kennedy's fidgeting hands during a rally in *Primary* (1960), which reveals how nervous she really is beneath her placid exterior (fig. 4.8).

Epstein and Balázs's true insight was that the cinema allows greater access to the minds of human beings than the other visual arts. However, they muddied this insight by wrongly conceiving of the nature of this access to the mind, comparing it to the revelation by visual technologies of phenomena the naked human eye is incapable of seeing unaided, when, in fact, people are perfectly capable of perceiving what others are thinking and feeling without assistance. What the cinema does do is *extend* this ability in ways the other visual arts cannot through variable framing, which can force the viewer to pay attention to details of the human face and body that can reveal much about their mental lives. Although painting, photography, and sculpture can do the same, as atemporal art forms they cannot do so as part of a succession of different views of the sort just described in which a truth is concealed at one moment and revealed at the next (and vice versa). And while the theater is, like the cinema, a temporal art, it lacks the control over the viewer's attention that the cinema possesses by way of editing and camera movement. In the hands of a great film artist such as Hitchcock, this control can be used to create a constantly changing drama of revelation and concealment.

Of course, films, and the agents in them, often exploit the limitations of human perception to hide things, and they often use visual technologies to overcome these limitations and thereby reveal them. Later in the scene from *Shadow of a Doubt* described above, young Charlie goes out to the garage to fetch the family car which her uncle has left running. He closes the window to the living room in which the family has gathered, complaining it is getting cold, and turns up the music playing on the radio so that the sounds of Charlie suffocating in the exhaust fumes will be masked. And when he first travels to Santa Rosa on a train, he conceals his identity by pretending to be ill and remaining behind a curtain in the passenger car. In both instances, he is exploiting the limitations of human perception to hide himself and his crimes. The police, meanwhile, use photography, a visual technology, to try to identify him. But the point remains that in these instances, what is being concealed—young Charlie

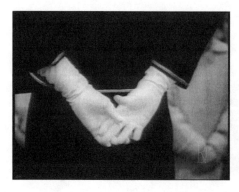

Figure 4.8. Jackie Kennedy's fidgeting hands reveal how nervous she really is in *Primary* (Robert Drew, 1960).

suffocating, Uncle Charlie's true identity—is capable of being perceived un-aided by human beings, which is why it is hidden in the first place.

Balázs, and especially Epstein, also point to the way in which the cinema can extend a type of seeing that is more typical of aesthetic practices than real life in order to reveal truths about human or humanlike agents. This is our abil-ity to see anthropomorphic properties in nonhuman entities—to see clouds, for example, as threatening, or a home as welcoming—which in films usually takes the form of endowing the environment around agents with expressive qualities using film style. The other visual arts also exploit this capacity. But, again, the cinema can do so in ways other visual arts cannot due to variable framing. In *Shadow of a Doubt,* when Charlie goes to the library to find an article that her uncle has surreptitiously removed from the family newspaper, she sits in the dark at a reading table, her face in profile in a medium close-up shot, the music quiet and expectant. It pauses for a brief second as she freezes, her gaze alight-ing on something. There follows a cut to a close-up from her point-of-view of a newspaper report about the merry widow murderer, accompanied by the merry widow waltz on the soundtrack, now rendered sinister by dramatic, loud, slow scoring in a minor key. The music quiets down again as Charlie examines the ring that her uncle gave her, which bears the initials of one of the murdered widows she has just read about. Then the camera pulls back and up in a virtuoso crane shot as Charlie slowly gets up from the table. Her figure, now seen from a high angle long shot, casts a shadow across the floor and onto the wall opposite, which grows in size and intensity as she walks toward the exit. The music gets louder again, and the camera climbs farther away from her, dwarfing her lonely figure (fig. 4.9). These techniques strongly encourage us to see the shadow as expressive of what Charlie is thinking and feeling: her dawning, horrific realiza-tion, which she hides from her family, that her beloved uncle is the merry widow murderer (they also perversely hint at her kinship with her uncle, who has been associated with shadows and the waltz throughout the film). These techniques illustrate how films can endow the environment around characters with expres-sive qualities that reveal their true cognitive and affective states even when the characters themselves do not explicitly express them verbally or physically.

Epstein realized that the cinema is an art with considerable expressive power. Yet, by assimilating the cinematic revelation of visible but hidden or

Figure 4.9. High-angle crane shot of Charlie as she leaves the library after discovering the truth about her uncle in *Shadow of a Doubt.*

unexpressed truths to the scientific revelation of inaccessible ones, he mis-construed it, arguing that it consists of making visible the "interior life" of objects, which human beings cannot see because we are confined to the ex-ternal appearances of things. In fact, we are quite capable of seeing a cloud as threatening or a home as welcoming without assistance. What the cinema does do is extend this ability by way of the numerous expressive techniques it has at its disposal, including ones not available to the other visual arts in their standard forms. For although other visual arts use many of the same expressive techniques as the cinema, they lack variable framing, which can be used for expressive purposes. In the above example, it is not just the shadow—a device the other visual arts could use—that expresses young Charlie's thoughts and feelings, but the fact that it grows in size and intensity as she becomes smaller in the frame due to the camera's movement away from her. This change in scale and bracketing brilliantly expresses both her isolation and her sense of being overwhelmed by her newfound knowledge.

In other films, Hitchcock uses stylistic techniques such as these for the op-posite reason—to conceal rather than reveal the truth about human beings. As Richard Allen has shown in meticulous detail, in *The Lodger* (1927) Hitchcock deceives the viewer by filming the lodger using expressionist techniques com-monly used to depict monsters and other evil characters in expressionist films of the 1920s, thereby suggesting that the lodger is the serial killer who is prey-ing upon young blonde women in London.[37] In fact, the lodger turns out to be the brother of one of the murdered women who seeks to avenge her death. This shows that filmmakers not only can reveal previously concealed truths, they can also play a game of hide-and-seek with the truth.[38] A good example is the filmmaker Jacques Tati, whose films are replete with subtle sight gags that the viewer not only has to work hard to notice because Tati refuses to direct our at-tention to them, but that Tati sometimes deliberately directs our attention away from and thereby conceals. In *Mon Oncle* (1958), there is a scene in which Tati's character Monsieur Hulot emerges with two friends from a neighborhood bar, one on either side. As he often does, Tati films the scene in a long shot and does not employ editing or other techniques to direct the viewer's attention to important information in the scene (fig. 4.10). The three men are grouped to the right of the shot, and as they converse, the man closest to the center moves to the left (fig. 4.11). At exactly the same moment, Hulot goes to tap his pipe on the heel of his shoe as he is accustomed to doing, only to discover that his shoe has accidentally slipped off and he is tapping the pipe on the heel of his foot (fig. 4.12). It is easy to overlook this gag because we are distracted by the much bigger and more noticeable movement of the man from right to left, which Tati has deliberately staged to occur at the same time as the pipe-tapping. When we notice a subtle sight gag such as this one in a Tati film, it is a revelation, not in the sense that something we are incapable of seeing unaided is made visible, but in the sense that we notice something it is easy to overlook.

As this example demonstrates, there is another sense of revelation perti-nent to cinematic art. Not only can films reveal what is invisible in the sense of bringing to view previously concealed truths, they can also draw our attention

Figure 4.10. Monsieur Hulot and friends leave a neighborhood bar in *Mon Oncle* (Jacques Tati, 1958).

Figure 4.11. As his friend moves screen left, Monsieur Hulot goes to tap his pipe on the heel of his shoe.

Figure 4.12. Monsieur Hulot discovers that his shoe has fallen off.

to truths that are in plain sight but that are invisible in the sense that we have not noticed or paid attention to them. Kracauer points to this type of visual revelation, although like other revelationist theorists he misconstrues it by comparing it to the revelation of natural phenomena we are incapable of seeing unaided. According to Kracauer, what we do not notice or pay attention to is the quotidian environment around us, which, due to the abstractness of modernity, we cannot see. Hence a visual technology is needed to reveal it. As I argued in chapter 2, to fail to attend to something is not to be incapable of seeing it without a visual technology. Indeed, in order to fail to attend to something, it must be capable of being attended to. However, once again there is a genuine insight buried in Kracauer's argument: the cinema is an art with an unparalleled capacity to direct our attention to truths that are in plain sight but that we do not notice or pay attention to, such as familiar environments. The other visual arts, of course, also possess this ability. However, variable framing and the control over attention it allows means that filmmakers can force us to notice things we might otherwise overlook. Stan Brakhage, for example, uses camera movement and editing to compel us to attend to details of our quotidian environment, thereby revealing its visual richness. A classic example in his films is light and shadow. He often draws our attention to the wide variety of shadows cast by objects, which we normally overlook because they are so familiar, by filming these shadows in close-up rather than the objects casting them (fig. 4.13). Watching a Brakhage film can be a revelation not in the sense that something we cannot see unaided is made visible, but in the sense that it makes us notice things—our environment's colors, textures, shapes, movements, and so on—that we see all the time but that we do not pay attention to due to their familiarity.

Revealing truths that we do not notice or pay attention to need not only involve what we see. It can also concern the way we see it. Films can make us notice the aesthetic conventions they use to shape the way we view them, as well as facts about perception these aesthetic conventions exploit. We are continuously exposed to these conventions, and the truths about perception they exploit are ones we take for granted. But we are typically not consciously aware of them until they are pointed out to us, just as we are usually unaware of the grammatical rules we follow when using language until they are pointed out to us by a grammarian. For example, filmmakers around the world tend to place the most important information at the center of a shot. This is a widespread aesthetic norm in the visual arts that exploits a fact about perception—we tend to look at the center of what we see, not its edges. Some filmmakers in the history of cinema, such as Tati, have systematically violated this norm by placing important information at the edge of the shot—the couple with a baby at the airport in the opening scene of *Playtime* (1967), for example (fig. 4.14). And in doing so, they can reveal to the viewer both this aesthetic convention and the feature

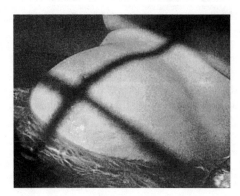

Figure 4.13. The shadow of a window on pregnant Jane Brakhage's abdomen in *Window Water Baby Moving* (Stan Brakhage, 1959).

of human perception it exploits in the sense of making the viewer notice or pay attention to them. Avant-garde films in particular traffic in this type of revelation, and they can offer a visual education in the sense that, by systematically contravening conventions, they force the viewer to notice the conventions filmmakers typically use to enable us to easily perceive the contents of an image. It is in this sense that the claim made by many avant-garde filmmakers that their films "reveal truths about perception" should be understood. They do not typically do so in the scientific sense of revealing invisible truths about perception we are incapable of seeing unaided, such as the fact that, when we see an object, imperceptible photons are absorbed by the photosensitive cells of the retina. Rather, they do so in the sense of making us aware of what we take for granted about perception and aesthetic conventions but do not pay attention to.

Of the four theorists in the revelationist tradition proper, only Vertov's examples of cinematic revelation genuinely involve bringing to view something that human sight is incapable of seeing unaided, although not in the way he supposed. Vertov, as a Marxist-Leninist, was not so much interested in truths about individuals as he was in the social relations between them. However, as we saw in chapter 2, due to his conflation of cinematic with scientific revelation, he tended to hypostatize such relations, to conceive of them as if they were intrinsic physical properties of an object we are incapable of seeing unaided, such as its particulate structure, rather than as relational properties possessed by virtue of interactions with the world. Furthermore, social relations of the sort Vertov was interested in revealing are not beyond the capacity of the human eye to perceive without assistance. We can, for example, see that two different people belong to the same class without the help of a visual technology by observing and comparing their interactions with the environment around them.

Nevertheless, as with the other theorists discussed, there is a profound insight about the cinema in Vertov's film theory: due to its capacity to record people in different times and places and to link these recordings together using editing, film can participate in what has been called "the expanding circle" of modernity to a much greater extent than the other arts.[39] "Expanding circle" refers to the way in which modern technologies of representation and travel can broaden the moral horizons of human beings beyond the traditional environment of family and village, in which everyone knows everyone else, to include unknown persons connected by geographical location, class, ethnicity, nation,

Figure 4.14. The couple with the baby in the bottom left of a shot in the opening scene of *Playtime* (Jacques Tati, 1967).

race, and ultimately humanity. Such technologies enable people to see, either directly or by way of recordings, what they have in common with others whom they have never met, thereby potentially extending their sense of moral responsibility beyond the people they know personally. Vertov, due to his political beliefs, was particularly concerned to use the cinema to show his working-class viewers what they have in common with workers whom they could never meet in person due to geographical distance, thereby fostering a sense of international working-class solidarity between them. As he put it, "We want to . . . give everyone working behind a plow or a machine the opportunity to see his brothers at work with him simultaneously in different parts of the world."[40]

Using the cinema to reveal what workers in different times and places have in common does not involve bringing to view something that is invisible in the sense that we are incapable of seeing it unaided, as Vertov tended to claim, for, as I have suggested, we can see without assistance that two people belong to the same class as well as seeing many other social relations. But the cinema can involve making *people* visible that we are incapable of perceiving unaided due to the fact that they are far away or lived a long time ago, thereby greatly enlarging the number of people with whom we can discover commonalities and thereby participate in the expanding circle of modernity. The cinema, in other words, vastly extends our capacity to observe what human beings have in common by recording people we would never be able to see without assistance and juxtaposing these recordings. This does not mean the cinema is more mobile than human perception and can move through time and space instantaneously, as Vertov and Deleuze claim, for a movie camera cannot travel into the past or future, and it has to be taken between places, which takes time. Instead, it is the transition between different shots recorded in different times and places that can be instantaneous (or not), and it is this, along with the cinema's recording capacity and the motion of its images, that allow its viewers to observe and compare people they would not be able to see otherwise. The other visual arts either lack editing, motion, recording, or all three. Hence, while they can connect people and reveal what they have in common, they cannot join separate, moving images of a wide variety of people recorded in a wide variety of times and places in the way that the cinema can.

In doing so, films can, once again, exploit a visual ability that the other visual arts also make use of, but that the cinema is able to extend in ways they cannot due to variable framing. As silent theorists and filmmakers such as Vertov quickly discovered, when filmed in a certain way, viewers can notice graphic properties of the cinematic image and its contents, such as shape, size, texture, and light. And films can utilize this ability by creating visual similarities and differences between the graphic properties of shots—as Vertov does in the sequence I discussed in chapter 1 comparing human being and machine—to suggest that the subjects of the shots have other properties in common, such as relational ones. *Shadow of a Doubt* provides a canonical example in the graphic similarities and differences Hitchcock creates between the scenes introducing Uncle Charlie and his niece.[41] In introducing Uncle Charlie, the film cuts to successively closer shots of a boarding house in a run-down neighborhood, the closest being a canted shot of one of its windows (fig. 4.15). Inside, we see Uncle Charlie lying on a bed, with the light from the lace curtains on his window reflected on the wall behind him as the camera dollies toward him (fig. 4.16). In introducing the niece Charlie, we see successively closer shots of her house from the opposite direction, following establishing shots of Santa Rosa with its safe, pleasant streets patrolled by friendly policemen. But the shot of her window is also canted (fig. 4.17), and when we cut inside, Charlie is lying in exactly the same position as her uncle with similar

Figure 4.15. A canted shot of Uncle Charlie's boarding-house bedroom window in *Shadow of a Doubt*.

Figure 4.16. Inside, Uncle Charlie lies on his bed, the shadows from the window curtains visible above him.

Figure 4.17. A canted shot of young Charlie's bedroom window.

shadows behind her, and the camera repeats the same forward dolly (fig. 4.18). By way of these visual similarities and differences, the attentive viewer will infer that Hitchcock is hinting that Uncle Charlie and his niece might have more in common than meets the eye. Indeed, through these graphic similarities and differences, Hitchcock is articulating the central question of the film (and, arguably, his work in general): does young Charlie have the same moral character as her uncle or not? Many of these graphic properties, such as the shadows and the position of the characters within the frame, are ones the other visual arts could make use of to reveal such relations. However, Hitchcock employs a cinematic property that they do not have at their disposal, variable framing, to do so. Each sequence employs the same camera movement, the forward dolly, as well as the same editing structure—successively closer shots— to hint at possible similarities between Charlie and her uncle. These techniques do not reveal something that we are incapable of seeing unaided, for we are quite capable of discovering without assistance whether two people are alike in character by observing and comparing their words and behavior. However, these techniques do encourage us to make this comparison, which we might neglect to do in their absence.

Thus arguing, as I have, that human vision is not limited to the extent that film theorists often claim does not mean that the cinema is incapable of revealing truths about reality that are invisible to the naked eye. Nor does it mean that it is unable to do so in ways the other arts cannot, at least as they are customarily practiced. However, its revelatory power is for the most part wrongly conceived of when it is compared exclusively to the scientific discovery of natural phenomena that human sight is incapable of seeing unaided. Although the technology of film can, like microscopes and telescopes, bring to view features of reality inaccessible to vision, this is not the only sense in which films reveal the invisible. Rather, as I have suggested, they also do so in the sense of revealing truths that we are capable of seeing unaided but that were previously concealed or that we did not pay attention to. And even when they do reveal things we cannot see without assistance, such as the workers in faraway places in Vertov's films, often this is in order to enable us to see things we are capable of perceiving without a visual technology, such as commonalities of class. Meanwhile, the difference between film and the other visual arts

Figure 4.18. Inside, young Charlie lies in the same position as her uncle with similar shadows above her.

lies principally in the way that it *extends* our visual capacities—our ability to see what other people are thinking and feeling, to see anthropomorphic properties in nonhuman entities, to see what we have in common with other people whom we have never met, to notice graphic properties as well as what we have overlooked—in ways they cannot due to variable framing.

Although theorists in the revelationist tradition correctly realized that the cinema's revelatory power is unparalleled among the arts in their standard forms, they misconstrued its nature because they likened it exclusively to scientific discoveries about invisible natural phenomena using visual technologies; this is not too surprising, given that our culture is a scientific one. The sciences have been so successful at explaining and predicting the natural universe over the last four centuries that they have become the paradigm of explanation in the modern world, thereby casting a long shadow over other types of knowledge, such as philosophy, religion, and art. The result has often been scientism, the illicit extension of the forms, methods, and rhetoric of the natural sciences into realms where they have no application in an effort to emulate their success. For this reason, theorists and practitioners of art have often clothed their work in scientific garb and compared artistic knowledge to scientific discovery.[42] In the case of the cinema, there is a particular temptation to do this, because film is a technology as well as an artistic medium and it can be used to make scientific discoveries about natural phenomena that we are incapable of seeing unaided.

Early theorists also misconstrued cinematic revelation, I suspect, because of the sheer novelty of seeing human faces, bodies, and environments on film. As Carroll has pointed out, variable framing, and the control over the viewer's attention it enables, results in a much greater degree of clarity in our experience of what is represented by a film than is possible in the theater or in real life. Through indexing, bracketing, and scaling, camera movement and editing enable the filmmaker to analyze what is filmed into variable views for the viewer, rendering it visually perspicuous. Of course, films don't have to use such techniques, and when they do, these techniques are not necessarily used to render their subjects perspicuous. But when these techniques are used in this way, the result can be "an element of cognitive clarity" that, as Carroll argues, "may well account . . . for the widespread intensity of engagement that movies elicit."[43] After more than a century of film, viewers are now accustomed to this clarity, but this was not the case with theorists in the revelationist tradition, who all grew to maturity while filmmakers were discovering and experimenting with the analytical techniques of variable framing. Due to the precision, detail, and proximity with which these techniques can allow viewers to observe reality, watching a film that used these techniques for the first time must have been like discovering a "world never seen before," as Kracauer puts it, much like the world of micro-phenomena revealed for the first time by microscopes. This is why, I suspect, they reached for the analogy with other visual technologies. As flawed as this analogy was, the insight about the cinema's unique revelatory power motivating it was sound.

In this book, I have attempted to show that skepticism about human vision has had a profound influence on film theorists since the 1920s and continues to do so. I have also offered a critique of this influence, arguing both that, in general, visual skepticism is probably unfounded, and that film theorists typically make skeptical arguments about vision at the price of misusing perceptual and related concepts. One thing that has struck me again and again when writing this book is that, even though the cinema is widely considered to be a visual art and theorizing about its visual properties has been going on for almost a century, film theorists are woefully confused about what it is we actually see when we watch films. The study of film badly needs philosophy to clarify precisely what it makes sense to say that a film viewer sees, in addition to close empirical study of the way films actually engage and artfully manipulate our sense of sight. Some film scholars, most notably David Bordwell, are doing the latter;[44] I hope here to have taken a few steps toward the former.

Nevertheless, I am pessimistic about the influence of skepticism about human vision on film theory coming to an end any time soon. The lure of visual skepticism, and the concomitant claim that the cinema can reveal truths about reality beyond the reach of human seeing and knowing, are too seductive. As I have suggested, film theorists are attracted to this conception of the cinema because it places film art on a par with science, philosophy, and other truth-seeking pursuits, thereby investing it with considerable status and moral value. But behind this conception, doesn't there lurk what Murray Smith has called "the ancient view that the worth of art will always pale in comparison with the worth of philosophy?"[45] Smith is referring to popular films such as comedies in arguing against the currently fashionable claim that films "philosophize," but his argument could apply to all films and all attempts to equate film art with nonartistic pursuits such as science and philosophy.

> A different path is open to us if we recognize and challenge this assumption. We can, and should, take popular films seriously—but as works of art, rather than as works of philosophy. After all, in the larger scheme of things, comic artistry is probably as important to human flourishing as philosophy. What it makes to take popular filmmaking as an art seriously, of course, is still another matter.[46]

Taking film as an art seriously involves clarifying what sort of knowledge *it* gives us, what sort of "truths about reality" *it* can reveal, rather than assimilating these truths to those of science or philosophy. I have suggested that it is, for the most part, truths about human beings and their environments that are invisible in the sense of being concealed or overlooked that the cinema as an art, as opposed to film as a technology, reveals. I suspect that such truths, to borrow Smith's felicitous phrase, are just as important to human flourishing as those scientific discoveries about natural phenomena that we are incapable of seeing unaided.

NOTES

INTRODUCTION

1. In this book, I use the term "classical film theory" solely for the purposes of historical periodization. The term refers to film theory produced before the Anglo-American academicization of film studies and the ascendancy of semiotic-psychoanalytical film theory in the late 1960s. Film theory since the late 1960s I refer to as "contemporary film theory." See Noël Carroll, *Philosophical Problems of Classical Film Theory* (Princeton, NJ: Princeton University Press, 1988), 10.

2. Ibid., 12–15.

3. Walter Benjamin, "The Work of Art in the Age of Mechanical Reproduction," in *Illuminations,* trans. Harry Zohn (New York: Schocken Books, 1969), 236.

4. Jean Epstein, "*Photogénie* and the Imponderable" (1935), in *French Film Theory and Criticism, A History/Anthology,* vol. II, *1929–1939,* ed. Richard Abel (Princeton, NJ: Princeton University Press, 1988), 190.

5. Béla Balázs, *Theory of the Film (Character and Growth of a New Art)* (1948), trans. Edith Bone (New York: Arno Press, 1972), 55.

6. Gregory Currie, "Visible Traces: Documentary and the Contents of Photographs," *Journal of Aesthetics and Art Criticism* 57, no. 3 (Summer 1999), 286.

7. See, for example, Annette Michelson, "The Wings of Hypothesis: On Montage and the Theory of the Interval," in *Montage and Modern Life 1919–1942,* ed. Matthew Teitelbaum (Cambridge, MA: MIT Press, 1992), 62; Richard Abel, "*Photogénie* and Company," in *French Film Theory and Criticism, A History/Anthology,* vol. I, *1907–1929,* ed. Richard Abel (Princeton, NJ: Princeton University Press, 1988), 107.

8. Alan Williams, *Republic of Images: A History of French Filmmaking* (Cambridge, MA: Harvard University Press, 1992), 58. Williams is referring here to the films of Dr. Jean Comandon in France. The cinema's revelatory capacity continues to have entertainment value today, as the recent documentary *Microcosmos* (1996) demonstrates.

9. Hugo Münsterberg, *The Film: A Psychological Study. The Silent Photoplay in 1916* (New York: Dover Publications, 1970), 11.

10. Jean Epstein, "The Cinema Continues" (1930), in *French Film Theory,* vol. II, 63–64.

11. Jean Epstein, "On Certain Characteristics of *Photogénie*" (1924), in *French Film Theory,* vol. I, 318.

12. Dziga Vertov, "Kinoks: A Revolution" (1923), in *Kino-Eye: The Writings of Dziga Vertov,* ed. Annette Michelson, trans. Kevin O'Brien (Berkeley: University of California Press, 1984), 17–18.

13. Dziga Vertov, "*Kinoglaz*" (1924), in *Kino-Eye,* 39.

14. Balázs, *Theory of the Film,* 33.

15. Ibid., 34–35.

16. Siegfried Kracauer, *Theory of Film: The Redemption of Physical Reality* (1960) (Princeton, NJ: Princeton University Press, 1997), 299, 300.

17. Ibid., 300.

18. Ibid., 296.

19. By our sense of sight, I should make clear immediately that I do not mean vision in any metaphorical or secondary sense, unlike, say, P. Adams Sitney, who has used vision as a metaphor for the imagination to argue that post-war American avant-garde film is "visionary." By this he means that its central theme is "the triumph of the imagination." In this tradition, according to Sitney, filmmakers employ "radical techniques" as "metaphors for perception and consciousness" (*Visionary Film: The American Avant-Garde 1943–2000* [Oxford: Oxford University Press, 2002], 65, 49). Nor do I mean that the cinema embodies or objectifies perceptual processes such as attention, which is what Hugo Münsterburg argued. Rather, for the filmmakers and theorists I analyze in this book, it is literal, physical vision, and the knowledge of reality we gain through seeing, that is limited.

20. In the pages that follow, I sometimes refer to this distrust of our sense of sight as skepticism. However, the use of the term skepticism should not be construed to mean modern, philosophical skepticism (i.e., doubts about the existence of reality and other minds), unless I indicate otherwise. Rather, I use "skepticism" in the more general sense of a doubting or questioning attitude toward sight. Indeed, the theorists and filmmakers I discuss have no doubt about the existence of reality and other minds because, according to them, the cinema has the power to escape the limitations of human vision and reveal reality and other minds as they really are.

21. David Bordwell, *French Impressionist Cinema: Film Culture, Film Theory, and Film Style* (New York: Arno Press, 1980); Stuart Liebman, "Jean Epstein's Early Film Theory, 1920–1922" (Ph.D. dissertation; New York University, 1980); Richard Abel, *French Cinema: The First Wave, 1915–1929* (Princeton, NJ: Princeton University Press, 1984); Jacques Aumont, ed., *Jean Epstein: Cinéaste, Poete, Philosophe* (Paris: Cinemateque Francaise, 1998); Vincent Guigueno, *Jean Epstein, cinéaste des îles: Ouessant, Sein, Hoëdic, Belle-Île* (Paris: Jean-Michel Place, 2003).

22. Joseph Zsuffa, *Béla Balázs: The Man and the Artist* (Berkeley: University of California Press, 1987); Sabine Hake, *Cinema's Third Machine: Writing on Film in Germany, 1907–1933* (Lincoln: University of Nebraska Press, 1993); Hanno Loewy, "Space, Time, and 'Rites de Passage': Béla Balázs's Paths to Film," *October* 115 (Winter 2006) and Loewy, *Béla Balázs: Marchen, Ritual, und Film* (Berlin: Vorwerk 8, 2003).

23. Annette Michelson, Introduction, *Kino-Eye;* Vlada Petric, *Constructivism in Film; The Man with the Movie Camera: A Cinematic Analysis* (Cambridge: Cambridge University Press, 1987); Yuri Tsivian, ed., *Lines of Resistance: Dziga Vertov and the*

Twenties (Sacile/Pordenone, Italy: Le Giornate del Cinema Muto, 2004); Thomas Tode and Barbara Wurm, *Dziga Vertov: The Vertov Collection at the Austrian Museum* (Vienna: Filmmuseum Synema Publikationen, 2006). John McKay summarizes the new wave of scholarship on Vertov in "The 'Spinning Top' Takes another Turn: Vertov Today," *KinoKultura* 8 (April 2005) [online]. Available: http://www.kinokultura.com/articles/apr05-mackay.html. See also Malcolm Turvey and Annette Michelson, eds., "New Vertov Studies," *October* 121 (Summer 2007).

24. See, for example, Thomas Y. Levin, Introduction to Siegfried Kracauer, *The Mass Ornament: Weimar Essays,* ed. and trans. Thomas Y. Levin (Cambridge, MA: Harvard University Press, 1995), 1–30.

25. Carroll, *Philosophical Problems,* 7.

26. Rudolf Arnheim, *Film as Art* (Berkeley: University of California Press, 1957), 35.

27. André Bazin, "The Ontology of the Photographic Image" (1945), in *What is Cinema?* vol. 1, trans. Hugh Gray (Berkeley: University of California Press, 1967), 14 (emphasis in original).

28. Ibid., 13–14.

29. Ibid., 15.

30. Linda Nochlin, *Realism* (New York: Penguin, 1971), 19.

31. André Bazin, "William Wyler, or the Jansenist of Directing" (1948), in *Bazin at Work,* ed. Bert Cardullo, trans. Alain Piette and Bert Cardullo (New York: Routledge, 1997), 7.

32. Vertov, "Kinoks," 15–16.

33. Dudley Andrew, *The Major Film Theories: An Introduction* (Oxford: Oxford University Press, 1976); Sabine Hake, *Cinema's Third Machine: Writing on Film in Germany, 1907–1933* (Lincoln: University of Nebraska Press, 1993), 213–14; Theodor W. Adorno, "The Curious Realist: On Siegfried Kracauer" (1965), *New German Critique* 54 (1991), 159–79.

34. The most persistent critic of medium specificity in film theory is Noël Carroll. See his essays "Medium Specificity Arguments and the Self-Consciously Invented Arts: Film, Video, and Photography"; "The Specificity of Media in the Arts"; "Concerning Uniqueness Claims for Photographic and Cinematographic Representation"; and "Defining the Moving Image," all in Carroll, *Theorizing the Moving Image* (Cambridge: Cambridge University Press, 1996), 1–74. Murray Smith has recently defended a version of medium specificity he calls "medium deflationism" against Carroll's criticisms. He argues that one can legitimately speak of the "cinematic" in the sense of features of a film that are "in some way *characteristic* or *prototypical* of the medium" (emphasis in original). See Smith, "My Dinner with Noël; or, Can We Forget the Medium?" *Film Studies: An International Review* 8 (Summer 2006), 146, and Carroll's response, "Engaging Critics," ibid., 161–63. Interestingly, Carroll also makes use of the idea of "characteristic" features in his essay "The Power of Movies" (also in *Theorizing the Moving Image,* 84). However, by this he means features typical of a certain genre—rather than the medium—of film, what he calls movies, by which he means mainstream narrative films.

35. Ludwig Wittgenstein, *Last Writings on the Philosophy of Psychology,* vol. 1, ed. G. H. von Wright and H. Nyman, trans. C. G. Luckhardt and M. A. E. Aue (Oxford: Blackwell, 1982), §885.

36. Annette Michelson, Introduction to *Kino-Eye,* xlvi.

37. Balázs, *Theory of the Film,* 75.

38. Kracauer, *Theory of Film,* 52.

39. Gilbert Ryle, *The Concept of Mind* (Chicago, IL: University of Chicago Press, 1949), 16.

40. The qualification "as they are customarily practiced" is important. In reconstructing some of the claims of the revelationist tradition about the cinema's revelatory capacity and the way it differentiates film from the other arts, I do not mean to replicate their medium-specific essentialism. The revelatory techniques that the cinema, I argue in chapter 4, does legitimately possess are ones the other arts do not have at their disposal in their standard forms. This does not mean they might not be able to develop equivalents of these techniques. Hence, these techniques should not be construed as being unique to the medium of film, but only unique to cinematic art as it is customarily practiced in relation to the other arts as they are customarily practiced. See Carroll, "The Power of Movies," 86–87.

41. For recent overviews and defenses of this tradition, see Oswald Hanfling, *Philosophy and Ordinary Language: The Bent and Genius of Our Tongue* (London: Routledge, 2000) and P. M. S. Hacker, *Wittgenstein's Place in Twentieth Century Analytic and Philosophy* (Oxford: Blackwell, 1996), especially chapters 6 through 8.

42. The following paragraphs are taken from Richard Allen and Malcolm Turvey, "Wittgenstein's Later Philosophy: A Prophylaxis against Theory," in *Wittgenstein, Theory and the Arts,* ed. Richard Allen and Malcolm Turvey (London: Routledge, 2001), 1–35.

43. Ludwig Wittgenstein, *Philosophical Investigations,* ed. G. E. M. Anscombe and R. Rhees, trans. G. E. M. Anscombe, 2nd ed. (Oxford: Blackwell, 1958), §109 (emphasis in original). (Hereafter cited in text as PI.)

44. Wittgenstein's distinction between the conceptual and the empirical has been challenged most prominently by W. V. Quine and his followers, who argue that all conceptualization is theory-ridden, and that there is no distinction between conceptual and empirical truths. For recent criticisms of this view and defenses of Wittgenstein, see H.-J. Glock, *Quine and Davidson on Language, Thought and Reality* (Cambridge: Cambridge University Press, 2003) and Hacker, *Wittgenstein's Place,* chapter 7.

45. Anthony Kenny, *The Metaphysics of Mind* (Oxford: Clarendon Press, 1989), 72–73.

46. Although Wittgenstein always contended that philosophical investigation is distinct from empirical enquiry and that the task of philosophy is the perspicuous characterization of meaning, he changed his mind about the nature of meaning during his lifetime with profound consequences. This is why his philosophy is usually divided into two periods, early and late. See Allen and Turvey, "Wittgenstein's Later Philosophy," 6–10.

47. Contemporary neuroscientists and neuroscientific philosophers of mind use this objection to defend their reckless application of psychological predicates to the brain. For criticisms, see M. R. Bennett and P. M. S. Hacker, *Philosophical Foundations of Neuroscience* (Oxford: Blackwell, 2003).

48. Epstein, *"Photogénie* and the Imponderable," 189.

49. Ibid.

50. Epstein, "The Cinema Continues," 64.

CHAPTER 1

1. Jean Epstein, "Magnification" (1921), in *French Film Theory and Criticism, A History/Anthology,* vol. I, *1907–1929,* ed. Richard Abel (Princeton, NJ: Princeton University Press, 1988), 240 (emphasis in original).

2. Ibid., 239–40.

3. Ibid., 240. With the coming of sound in the late 1920s, Epstein abandons his view that the cinema is, or should be, an exclusively visual art.

4. Henri Bergson, *Matter and Memory,* trans. N. M. Paul and W. S. Palmer (New York: Zone Books, 1988), 208.

5. Ibid.

6. Jean Epstein, "*Photogénie* and the Imponderable" (1935), in *French Film Theory and Criticism, A History/Anthology,* vol. II, *1929–1939,* ed. Richard Abel (Princeton, NJ: Princeton University Press, 1988), 189.

7. Epstein, "Magnification," 235.

8. Jean Epstein, "The Senses I (b)" (1921), in *French Film Theory,* vol. I, 244–45.

9. Epstein, "*Photogénie* and the Imponderable," 190.

10. Ibid.

11. Jean Epstein, "On Certain Characteristics of *Photogénie*" (1924), in *French Film Theory,* vol. I, 317.

12. Jean Epstein, "The Cinema Continues" (1930), in *French Film Theory,* vol. II, 64.

13. Alfred North Whitehead, *Science and the Modern World* (New York: Free Press, 1967), 54.

14. Epstein, "The Senses," 244.

15. Ibid.

16. Bergson, *Matter and Memory,* 10.

17. Ibid., 33.

18. Ibid., 35–36.

19. Ibid., 36.

20. Henri Bergson, *Creative Evolution,* trans. Arthur Mitchell (Mineola, NY: Dover Publications, 1998), 12 (emphasis in original).

21. Bergson, *Matter and Memory,* 49.

22. Ibid., 30–31.

23. Ibid., 49.

24. Ibid., 36.

25. Bergson, *Creative Evolution,* 306.

26. Ibid., xii.

27. Stuart Liebman, "Jean Epstein's Early Film Theory, 1920–1922" (Ph.D. dissertation, New York University, 1980), 149.

28. William R. Paulson, *Enlightenment, Romanticism, and the Blind in France* (Princeton, NJ: Princeton University Press, 1987), 150.

29. Epstein, "On Certain Characteristics of *Photogénie,*" 316–17.

30. Epstein, "For a New Avant-Garde" (1925), in Abel, *French Film Theory,* vol. I, 352.

31. Epstein, "Magnification," 238.

32. Kristin Thompson and David Bordwell, for example, include it in their list of Impressionist films in their *Film History: An Introduction* (New York: McGraw Hill, 2003), 89.

33. Richard Abel, *French Cinema: The First Wave, 1915–1929* (Princeton, NJ: Princeton University Press, 1984), 471: "Although *Usher* seems to announce a break in Epstein's aesthetic commitment, the effect of that break remains unarticulated."

34. Dziga Vertov, "We: Variant of a Manifesto" (1922), in *Kino-Eye: The Writings of Dziga Vertov,* ed. Annette Michelson, trans. Kevin O'Brien (Berkeley: University of California Press, 1984), 7.

35. Dziga Vertov, "On the Significance of Nonacted Cinema" (1923), in *Kino-Eye,* 36.

36. El Lissitzky, "Russia: The Reconstruction of Architecture in the Soviet Union" (excerpt), in *The Tradition of Constructivism,* ed. Stephen Bann (New York: Da Capo Press, 1990), 142.

37. Dziga Vertov, "On the Film Known as *Kinoglaz*" (1923), in *Kino-Eye,* 35.

38. Dziga Vertov, "Artistic Drama and Kino-Eye" (1924), in *Kino-Eye,* 48.

39. Dziga Vertov, "Kinoks: A Revolution" (1923), in *Kino-Eye,* 16.

40. Ibid., 14.

41. Ibid., 19.

42. Ibid., 16.

43. Ibid., 15.

44. Dziga Vertov, "The Birth of Kino-Eye" (1924), in *Kino-Eye,* 42.

45. Dziga Vertov, "*Kinoglaz*" (1924), in *Kino-Eye,* 39.

46. Vertov, "Kinoks," 16.

47. Vertov, "Kino-Eye" (1926), in *Kino-Eye,* 73.

48. Vertov, "Kinoks," 18–19 (emphasis added).

49. Vertov, "We," 8–9 (emphasis in original).

50. Vertov, "Kinoks," 16.

51. Ibid., 15, 18.

52. Ibid., 18.

53. Ibid., 17.

54. Ibid., 19.

55. Vertov, "Birth of Kino-Eye," 41.

56. Richard Stites, *Revolutionary Dreams: Utopian Vision and Experimental Life in the Russian Revolution* (New York: Oxford University Press, 1989), chapter 7.

57. See Malcolm Turvey, "Can the Camera See? Mimesis in *Man with a Movie Camera,*" *October* 89 (Summer 1999), 25–50.

58. Vertov, "We," 7–8 (emphasis in original).

59. Hillary Fink, *Bergson and Russian Modernism, 1900–1930* (Evanston, IL: Northwestern University Press, 1999). I explore the possible influence of Bergson on Vertov in Turvey, "Vertov: Between the Organism and the Machine," *October* 121, "New Vertov Studies," ed. Malcolm Turvey and Annette Michelson (Summer 2007).

60. Gilles Deleuze, *Cinema 1: The Movement Image,* trans. Hugh Tomlinson and Barbara Habberjam (1983; Minneapolis: University of Minnesota Press, 1986), 81.

61. Ibid., 39.

62. Ibid., 80.

63. Ibid., 40.

64. Ibid., 81.

65. John McKay, "A Superhuman Eye," section 1 of "Disorganized Noise: *Enthusiasm* and the Ear of the Collective," 7 [online] January 2005. Available: http://www.kinokultura.com/articles/enthusiasm-noise.pdf. The fragile, even contradictory balance between human and machine in Vertov's theory and practice is discussed in Turvey, "Can the Camera See?"

66. Béla Balázs, *Theory of the Film (Character and Growth of a New Art)* (1948), trans. Edith Bone (New York: Arno Press, 1972), 39. (Hereafter cited in the text as TTF.) *Theory of the Film* was originally published in 1948 in Hungary as *Filmkultúra* and translated into English in 1952. According to Joseph Zsuffa, it is a "common misconception" that *Filmkultúra* is the same as *Iskusstvo Kino,* published in Russia in 1945 (*Béla Balázs: The Man and the Artist* [Berkeley: University of California Press, 1987],

496, n. 69). "While parts of the two editions correspond, *Filmkultúra* is a different book."

67. Rudolf Arnheim, *Art and Visual Perception: A Psychology of the Creative Eye* (Berkeley: University of California Press, 1960), v–vi.

68. Siegfried Kracauer, *Theory of Film: The Redemption of Physical Reality* (1960) (Princeton, NJ: Princeton University Press, 1997), 46. (Hereafter cited in the text as TF.)

69. Quoted in David Frisby, *Fragments of Modernity: Theories of Modernity in the Work of Simmel, Kracauer and Benjamin* (Cambridge, MA: MIT Press, 1986), 112.

70. See Noël Carroll, *Philosophical Problems of Classical Film Theory* (Princeton, NJ: Princeton University Press, 1988), chapter 1; and David Bordwell, *On the History of Film Style* (Cambridge, MA: Harvard University Press, 1997), chapter 2.

71. For a critique of Kracauer's claims about cinema's medium-specific properties, see Noël Carroll, "Kracauer's *Theory of Film*," in *Defining Cinema,* ed. Peter Lehman (New Brunswick, NJ: Rutgers University Press, 1997), 111–31.

72. Siegfried Kracauer, "Cult of Distraction" (1927), in *The Mass Ornament: Weimar Essays,* ed. and trans. Thomas Y. Levin (Cambridge, MA: Harvard University Press, 1995), 326 (emphasis in original).

73. Ibid., 327.

74. Miriam Hansen, Introduction to Kracauer, *Theory of Film,* xiii.

75. Alfred North Whitehead, *Science and the Modern World* (New York: Free Press, 1967), 16.

76. Ibid., 35.

77. Daniel Belgrad, *The Culture of Spontaneity: Improvisation and the Arts in Postwar America* (Chicago: University of Chicago Press, 1998), 120–41.

78. Whitehead, *Science and the Modern World,* 196.

79. Ibid., 197.

80. Ibid., 199.

CHAPTER 2

1. Henri Bergson, *Creative Evolution,* trans. Arthur Mitchell (Mineola, NY: Dover Publications, 1998), 4.

2. Ibid., 3.

3. Ibid., 5 (emphasis in original).

4. Jean Epstein, "*Photogénie* and the Imponderable" (1935), in *French Film Theory and Criticism, A History/Anthology,* vol. II, *1929–1939,* ed. Richard Abel (Princeton, NJ: Princeton University Press, 1988), 189.

5. Ibid.

6. Epstein, "Magnification" (1921), in *French Film Theory and Criticism, A History/Anthology,* vol. I, *1907–1929,* ed. Richard Abel (Princeton, NJ: Princeton University Press, 1988), 236.

7. Jean Epstein, "The Senses I (b)" (1921), in *French Film Theory,* vol. 1, 242.

8. Jean Epstein, "Art of Incidence" (1927), in *French Film Theory,* vol. 1, 413.

9. Ibid., 413–14.

10. See *The Philosophy of Time: A Collection of Essays,* ed. Richard Gale (Garden City, NY: Anchor Books, 1967), 5–8.

11. Ludwig Wittgenstein, *The Blue and Brown Books* (Oxford: Blackwell, 1958), 26.

12. Ibid., 6.

13. Arthur S. Eddington, *The Nature of the Physical World* (New York: Macmillan, 1929), x.

14. Gilbert Ryle, *Dilemmas* (Cambridge: Cambridge University Press, 1954), chapter 5.

15. Ibid., 79 (emphasis in original).

16. P. M. S. Hacker, *Appearance and Reality: A Philosophical Investigation into Perception and Perceptual Qualities* (Oxford: Blackwell, 1987), 204.

17. Dziga Vertov, "The Birth of Kino-Eye" (1924), in *Kino-Eye: The Writings of Dziga Vertov,* ed. Annette Michelson, trans. Kevin O'Brien (Berkeley: University of California Press, 1984), 41.

18. Dziga Vertov, "On the Film Known as *Kinoglaz*" (1923), in *Kino-Eye,* 35.

19. Annette Michelson, "From Magician to Epistemologist: Vertov's *The Man with a Movie Camera,*" in *The Essential Cinema,* ed. P. Adams Sitney (New York: New York University Press, 1975), 104.

20. Vertov, "On the Film Known as *Kinoglaz,*" 34.

21. Ibid.

22. Annette Michelson, Introduction to *Kino-Eye,* xxxvii.

23. Ibid.

24. Ibid.

25. Ryle, *Dilemmas,* 86.

26. Ibid., 88.

27. Epstein, "Magnification," 238–39.

28. Ibid., 238.

29. Jean Epstein, "On Certain Characteristics of *Photogénie*" (1924), in *French Film Theory,* vol. 1, 317.

30. Ibid.

31. Ibid.

32. Epstein, "The Senses I (b)," 242.

33. Jean Epstein, "For a New Avant-Garde," in *French Film Theory,* vol. 1, 352.

34. Ibid.

35. Epstein, "*Photogénie* and the Imponderable," 191.

36. Ibid.

37. Ludwig Wittgenstein, *Philosophical Investigations,* ed. G. E. M. Anscombe and R. Rhees, trans. G. E. M. Anscombe, 2nd ed. (Oxford: Blackwell, 1958), 196. (Hereafter cited in the text as PI.)

38. Hacker, *Appearance and Reality,* 19 (emphasis in original).

39. Ludwig Wittgenstein, *Remarks on the Philosophy of Psychology,* vol. 2, ed. G. H. von Wright and H. Nyman, trans. C. G. Luckhardt and M. A. E. Aue (Oxford: Blackwell, 1980), §570 (emphasis in original).

40. For an in-depth examination of the issues covered in the following paragraphs, see Stephen Mulhall, *On Being in the World: Wittgenstein and Heidegger on Seeing Aspects* (London: Routledge, 1990). My discussion of aspect-dawning is greatly indebted to this book.

41. Béla Balázs, *Theory of the Film (Character and Growth of a New Art)* (1948), trans. Edith Bone (New York: Arno Press, 1972), 60 (emphasis in original). (Hereafter cited in the text as TTF.)

42. Anthony Kenny, *The Metaphysics of Mind* (Oxford: Clarendon Press, 1989), 5.

43. For this reason, Wittgenstein's philosophy of psychology has often been mistaken for a form of logical behaviorism. But unlike behaviorists, Wittgenstein does not argue that mental concepts can be reduced to behavior. See Paul Johnston, *Wittgenstein:*

Rethinking the Inner (London: Routledge, 1993); P. M. S. Hacker, *Wittgenstein: Meaning and Mind, Volume 3 of an Analytical Commentary on the Philosophical Investigations, Part 1: Essays* (Oxford: Blackwell, 1993), especially chapter 6; and Kenny, *Metaphysics of Mind*, 1–6.

44. Siegfried Kracauer, *Theory of Film: The Redemption of Physical Reality* (1960) (Princeton, NJ: Princeton University Press, 1997), 299. (Hereafter cited in the text as TF.)

45. Standish D. Lawder, *The Cubist Cinema* (New York: New York University Press, 1975), 72.

CHAPTER 3

1. Of course, there are important exceptions, such as Theodor Adorno and Max Horkheimer. See their "The Culture Industry: Enlightenment as Mass Deception" (1947), in Adorno and Horkheimer, *Dialectic of Enlightenment* (London: Verso, 1997), 120–167.

2. See, for example, Siegfried Kracauer's analysis of the antiliberal ideology in German cinema between the wars in *From Caligari to Hitler: A Psychological History of the German Film* (1947) (Princeton, NJ: Princeton University Press, 1990). Again, there are important exceptions, such as Vertov, who, in proselytizing on behalf of nonfiction film, tends to argue that fiction film in general, rather than specific fiction films, "clouds the eye and the brain with a sweet fog" (Dziga Vertov, "Artistic Drama and Kino-Eye" [1924], in *Kino-Eye: The Writings of Dziga Vertov*, ed. Annette Michelson, trans. Kevin O'Brien [Berkeley: University of California Press, 1984], 48).

3. For a critique of the attribution of ideology to the cinema's basic properties, see Noël Carroll, *Mystifying Movies: Fads and Fallacies in Contemporary Film Theory* (New York: Columbia University Press, 1988), chapters 3–5.

4. Because this theoretical terrain is well known, and others have surveyed it in much more detail than I have room to do here, I will only briefly summarize it as far as it pertains to my argument. An excellent, philosophically informed overview can be found in chapters 1 and 2 of Richard Allen, *Projecting Illusion: Film Spectatorship and the Impression of Reality* (Cambridge: Cambridge University Press, 1995).

5. Louis Althusser, "Ideology and Ideological State Apparatuses (Notes Toward an Investigation)," in Althusser, *Lenin and Philosophy and Other Essays*, trans. Ben Brewster (New York: Monthly Review Press, 1971), 85–127.

6. Allen, *Projecting Illusion*, 28.

7. Jacques Lacan, "The Mirror Stage as Formative of the Function of the I," in Lacan, *Écrits: A Selection*, trans. Alan Sheridan (New York: Tavistock Publications, 1977), 1–7.

8. Althusser, "Ideology"; see also Althusser, "Freud and Lacan," in *Lenin and Philosophy*, 133–51.

9. Lacan, "The Mirror Stage."

10. Bertolt Brecht, "Alienation Effects in Chinese Acting" (1936), in *Brecht on Theatre: The Development of an Aesthetic*, ed. and trans. John Willett (New York: Hill and Wang, 1964), 91–92.

11. Christian Metz, *The Imaginary Signifier: Psychoanalysis and the Cinema*, trans. Celia Britton et al. (Bloomington: Indiana University Press, 1982), 45.

12. Ibid., 49 (emphasis in original).

13. Ibid., 48 (emphasis in original).

14. Charles Taylor, *Sources of the Self: The Making of the Modern Identity* (Cambridge, MA: Harvard University Press, 1989), 420.

15. P. Adams Sitney has pointed to the autotelic nature of American structural film:

The structural film . . . has the same relationship to the earlier forms of the avant-garde film that Symbolism had to its source, Romanticism. The rhetoric of inspiration has changed to the language of aesthetics; Promethean heroism collapses into a consciousness of the self in which its very representation becomes problematic; the quest for a redeemed innocence becomes a search for the purity of images and the trapping of time. All this is as true of structural film as it is of Symbolism. (Sitney, *Visionary Film: The American Avant-Garde 1943–2000* [Oxford: Oxford University Press, 2002], 355.)

16. Stephen Heath, "Repetition Time: Notes around 'Structural/materialist Film'" (1978), in Heath, *Questions of Cinema* (Bloomington: Indiana University Press, 1981), 165 (emphasis in original).

17. Ibid., 167.

18. Noël Carroll, *The Philosophy of Horror, or, Paradoxes of the Heart* (New York: Routledge, 1990), 64.

19. For additional arguments, see Carroll, *Mystifying Movies,* chapter 3.

20. Allen, *Projecting Illusion,* 82.

21. Ibid, 100.

22. Ibid., 106–7.

23. There are illusions we can choose to experience indirectly. There are trompe-l'oeils, for example, that, when viewed from a certain distance, deceive us into believing we are in the presence of what they depict. When we move close enough to them, we can see their surfaces, and the illusion evaporates. We can then return to the position from which we originally saw them. Because we can no longer see their surfaces they appear, once again, to be the things they depict rather than representations, even though they no longer cognitively deceive us into believing they are real because we have seen their surfaces and know they are illusions. There might even be trompe-l'oeils that, when we look at part of them (the center), appear to be what they depict, but when we look at another part (the edges), are plainly representations. In these cases, we do, indirectly, choose to experience a perceptual illusion in the sense that we choose the optimum position in space, or the optimum part of the illusion to look at, in order to trigger the illusion. We, in effect, help the illusion to deceive our eyes. Perhaps such an experience could be made to occur in the cinema by, for example, placing viewers far enough away from the screen so that they cannot tell whether they are seeing a representation or something real, or by eschewing conventions such as editing, camera movement, titles, and music that would alert them to the fact that they are seeing a representation. But this is not how films are usually exhibited or designed.

24. Allen, *Projecting Illusion,* 88.

25. Stanley Cavell, *The World Viewed,* enlarged edition (Cambridge, MA: Harvard University Press, 1979), 22.

26. Ibid., 23.

27. Ibid., 24.

28. Ibid., 25–26.

29. William Rothman and Marian Keane, *Reading Cavell's The World Viewed: A Philosophical Perspective on Film* (Detroit, MI: Wayne State University Press, 2000), 180.

30. Cavell, *The World Viewed,* 102 (emphasis in original).

31. Ibid., 23.

32. Ibid., 19–20.

33. David Bordwell, *On the History of Film Style* (Cambridge, MA: Harvard University Press, 1997), 141–46; Charlie Keil, " 'To Here from Modernity': Style, Historiography, and Transitional Cinema," in *American Cinema's Transitional Era: Audiences, Institutions, Practices,* ed. Charlie Keil and Shelly Stamp (Berkeley: University of California Press, 2004), 51–65.

34. Ben Singer, *Melodrama and Modernity: Early Sensational Cinema and Its Contexts* (New York: Columbia University Press, 2001), 104.

35. Jonathan Crary, *Techniques of the Observer: On Vision and Modernity in the Nineteenth Century* (Cambridge, MA: MIT Press, 1990), 20.

36. Siegfried Kracauer, "Cult of Distraction" (1927), in *The Mass Ornament: Weimar Essays,* ed. and trans. Thomas Y. Levin (Cambridge, MA: Harvard University Press, 1995), 326 (emphasis in original).

37. Tom Gunning, "An Aesthetic of Astonishment: Early Film and the Incredulous Spectator" (1989), in *Film Theory and Criticism: Introductory Readings,* ed. Leo Braudy and Marshall Cohen, 6th ed. (Oxford: Oxford University Press, 2004), 875.

38. Miriam Hansen, "The Mass Production of the Senses: Classical Cinema as Vernacular Modernism," in *Reinventing Film Studies,* ed. Christine Gledhill and Linda Williams (London: Arnold, 2000), 341–42.

39. Kracauer, "The Cult of Distraction," 325–26.

40. Ibid., 327.

41. Ibid., 328.

42. Walter Benjamin, "The Work of Art in the Age of Mechanical Reproduction" (1935), in *Illuminations,* ed. Hannah Arendt (New York: Schocken, 1968), 238 (emphasis added).

43. Ibid. I develop my critique of the modernity thesis further in chapter 1 of Turvey, *The Filming of Modern Life* (Cambridge, MA: MIT Press, forthcoming).

44. Gilles Deleuze, *Cinema 1: The Movement Image* (1983), trans. Hugh Tomlinson and Barbara Habberjam (Minneapolis: University of Minnesota Press, 1986), 2.

45. Ibid., 64.

46. Ibid., 58, 64.

47. Ibid., 29.

48. Gilles Deleuze, *Cinema 2: The Time-Image* (1985), trans. Hugh Tomlinson and Robert Galeta (Minneapolis: University of Minnesota Press, 1989), xi.

49. Ibid., 274. See also p. 81.

50. Ibid., 101.

51. Ibid., xii.

52. Deleuze, *Cinema 1,* 63–64.

53. Ludwig Wittgenstein, *Philosophical Investigations,* ed. G. E. M. Anscombe and R. Rhees, trans. G. E. M. Anscombe, 2nd ed. (Oxford: Blackwell, 1958), §281. (Hereafter cited in the text as PI.)

54. Deleuze, *Cinema 1,* 20.

55. Anthony Kenny, *The Metaphysics of Mind* (Oxford: Clarendon Press, 1989), 106.

56. Deleuze, *Cinema 2,* xii.

57. See Currie's discussion of cinema and time in his *Image and Mind: Film, Philosophy, and Cognitive Science* (Cambridge: Cambridge University Press, 1995), 92–103.

58. Shorn of this extravagant theoretical claim, Deleuze's work on the cinema is little more than a history of film, one that, as David Bordwell has pointed out, is in

almost all respects traditional and derivative of the work of others. Bordwell, *Film Style,* 116–17.

CHAPTER 4

1. Rosalind Krauss, *The Optical Unconscious* (Cambridge, MA: MIT Press, 1993).

2. Ibid., 15, 19 (emphasis in original).

3. Ibid., 82–88.

4. Martin Jay, *Downcast Eyes: The Denigration of Vision in Twentieth-Century French Thought* (Berkeley: University of California Press, 1993), 14, 69.

5. Ibid.; see 154ff for Jay's discussion of Impressionism and post-Impressionism.

6. Jonathan Crary, *Techniques of the Observer: On Vision and Modernity in the Nineteenth Century* (Cambridge, MA: MIT Press, 1990), 39.

7. Ibid., 70.

8. A good overview of many of these views is given by Howard Robinson, *Perception* (London: Routledge, 1994).

9. The argument that follows pertains only to *artistic* modernism, and when I use the word "modernism," it should be understood as referring only to modernism of the artistic variety. I am not making any claims about modernity, as do Jay and Crary, nor about the arts in general. My claim pertains only to the modernist movement within the arts.

10. P. Adams Sitney, *Modernist Montage: The Obscurity of Vision in Cinema and Literature* (New York: Columbia University Press, 1990), 1.

11. Ibid., 2.

12. Ibid., 3.

13. Roman Jakobson, "Futurism" (1919), in *Language in Literature,* ed. Krystyna Pomorska and Stephen Rudy (Cambridge, MA.: Belknap Press, 1987), 32.

14. Lee T. Lemon and Marion J. Reiss, Introduction to Victor Shklovsky, "Art as Technique," in *Russian Formalist Criticism: Four Essays,* trans. Lee T. Lemon and Marion J. Reis (Lincoln: University of Nebraska Press, 1965), 4.

15. Walter Benjamin, "The Work of Art in the Age of Mechanical Reproduction," in *Illuminations,* trans. Harry Zohn (New York: Schocken Books, 1969).

16. For Léger's relation to classicism, see Christopher Green's *Léger and the Avant-Garde* (New Haven, CT: Yale University Press, 1976).

17. Fernand Léger, "The Spectacle: Light, Color, Moving Image, Object-Spectacle" (1924), in *Functions of Painting* (New York: Viking Press, 1973), 46.

18. Ibid., 47. I explore these issues further in Turvey, "The Avant-Garde and the 'New Spirit': The Case of Ballet Mécanique," *October* 102 (Fall 2002).

19. M. H. Abrams, *Natural Supernaturalism, Tradition and Revolution in Romantic Literature* (New York: W. W. Norton & Company, 1971), 377.

20. Stan Brakhage, "Metaphors on Vision" (extract), in *The Avant-Garde Film: A Reader of Theory and Criticism,* ed. P. Adams Sitney (New York: Anthology Film Archives, 1978), 120–21.

21. William C. Wees, *Light Moving in Time: Studies in the Visual Aesthetics of Avant-Garde Film* (Berkeley: University of California Press, 1992), 79.

22. P. Adams Sitney, *Visionary Film: The American Avant-Garde 1943–2000* (Oxford: Oxford University Press, 2002), 168.

23. Maurice Tuchman, "Hidden Meanings in Abstract Art," in *The Spiritual in Art: Abstract Painting 1890–1985,* exhibition catalogue (New York: Abbeville Press, 1986), 19.

24. Sixten Ringbom, "Transcending the Visible: The Generation of the Abstract Pioneers," in *The Spiritual in Art,* 131–54.

25. Linda Dalrymple Henderson, *The Fourth Dimension and Non-Euclidean Geometry in Modern Art* (Princeton, NJ: Princeton University Press, 1983), 340.

26. For criticisms of this picture, see Gilbert Ryle, *Dilemmas* (Cambridge: Cambridge University Press, 1954), chapter 5; P. M. S. Hacker, *Appearance and Reality: A Philosophical Investigation into Perception and Perceptual Qualities* (London: Blackwell, 1987). See Robinson, *Perception,* for a good overview of the variety of possible positions.

27. Sitney, *Modernist Montage,* 1.

28. Charles Taylor, *Sources of the Self: The Making of the Modern Identity* (Cambridge, MA: Harvard University Press, 1989), 419.

29. Ryle, *Dilemmas,* 94.

30. Ludwig Wittgenstein, *On Certainty,* trans. Denis Paul and G. E. M. Anscombe (New York: Harper & Row, 1972). (Hereafter cited in the text as OC.)

31. For further elaboration, see Turvey, "Is Scepticism a Natural Possibility of Language?: Reasons to be Sceptical of Cavell's Wittgenstein," in *Wittgenstein, Theory and the Arts,* ed. Richard Allen and Malcolm Turvey (London: Routledge, 2001), 117–36.

32. Ludwig Wittgenstein, *Zettel,* ed. G. E. M. Anscombe and G. H. von Wright, trans. G. E. M. Anscombe (Oxford: Blackwell, 1967), §571 (emphasis in original).

33. Ryle, *Dilemmas,* 95–96.

34. Patrick Maynard conceives of photography in this way in his *Engine of Visualization: Thinking Through Photography* (Ithaca, NY: Cornell University Press, 2000).

35. P. M. S. Hacker, *Wittgenstein: Meaning and Mind, Volume 3 of an Analytical Commentary on the Philosophical Investigations, Part 1: Essays* (Oxford: Blackwell, 1993), 134. My discussion of psychological concepts in this chapter is greatly indebted to this book.

36. Noël Carroll, "The Power of Movies," in *Theorizing the Moving Image* (Cambridge: Cambridge University Press), 84–87.

37. Richard Allen, "*The Lodger* and the Origins of Hitchcock's Aesthetic," *Hitchcock Annual* (2001–2002), 38–78.

38. See Thomas M. Leitch, *Find the Director and Other Hitchcock Games* (Athens: University of Georgia Press, 1991).

39. The term originates in the work of the nineteenth-century historian W. H. Lecky. It has been taken up most famously by the moral philosopher Peter Singer. See his *The Expanding Circle: Ethics and Sociobiology* (Oxford: Oxford University Press, 1981).

40. Dziga Vertov, "Kino-Eye" (1926), in *Kino-Eye: The Writings of Dziga Vertov,* ed. Annette Michelson, trans. Kevin O'Brien (Berkeley: University of California Press, 1984), 73–74.

41. James McLaughlin, "All in the Family: Alfred Hitchcock's *Shadow of a Doubt,*" in *A Hitchcock Reader,* ed. Marshall Deutelbaum and Leland Poague (Ames: Iowa State University Press, 1986), 141–52.

42. On this topic, see Paisley Livingston, *Literary Knowledge: Humanistic Inquiry and the Philosophy of Science* (Ithaca, NY: Cornell University Press, 1988).

43. Carroll, "The Power of Movies," 84.

44. See, for example, David Bordwell, *Figures Traced in Light: On Cinematic Staging* (Berkeley: University of California Press, 2005).

45. Murray Smith, "Film Art, Argument, and Ambiguity," *The Journal of Aesthetics and Art Criticism* 64, no. 1 (Winter 2006), 41.

46. Ibid.

INDEX